IRON MEN WITH GOLDEN HEARTS IN WOODEN SHIPS

A collection of stories of the brave Saban men of the sea.

Raymond S. Simmons II
with Will Johnson

Published by
Raymond Stanley Simmons II
7501 Citrus Ave., #934
Goldenrod, FL 32733
United States of America

First Edition: July 2014
Photos digitally enhanced by: Raymond S. Simmons II

Book cover design, format & layout by Artygraphic LLC – Oviedo, FL USA
Printed in United States of America

Publication made possible thanks to financial support from the Prins Bernhard Cultuurfonds Caribisch Gebied

Prins Bernhard / Cultuurfonds
CARIBISCH GEBIED

Table of Contents

FOREWORD

O ver the many years of doing research and publishing books and articles about the lives of the people of Saba, you always feel that there is still much more to be found and written about. This book of Raymond Simmons, a descendant of Saban shipbuilders and captains, certainly fills in a void which has existed. The glory period of Saba's history is, for a large part, written in the lives and the loss of lives of the many island men who went down to the sea and ventured out on the oceans seas in boats built on our small island.

For the past few centuries, writers in other countries have been writing about our little island and provided their readers with many fanciful stories about ships being built in the crater of the volcano and lowered over the cliffs into the sea.

Many of these writers have never even visited Saba, but their stories went on to acquire lives of their own and were quoted even into modern times as having taken place. Over the years, through oral history and backed up by research, we were able to prove them wrong and give an accurate history of our small island and the men and women who lived here and went on to do well in many countries after they left Saba.

Raymond has concentrated his research on a number of Saba islanders who wrestled with the elements and went on to become Captains and sailed all over the world. In their old age they returned to their native island to tell tales of going around Cape Horn, sailing to Australia, Africa, China and wherever there was trade and also to take part in the wars in the countries where they lived. I can still recall when visiting my aunt Alice Simmons and her husband Uncle Stanley Johnson in Richmond Hill, in the winter of 1967 and him telling me: "This cold is nothing. You should have experienced Murmansk in World War II when I used to carry supplies there for the Russians." And he would proceed to regale me with tales of his and other Saban's experiences during those two world wars of the previous century.

For this brief introduction I would like to bring one example of how our people fought the elements and, in this case, had a miraculous survival.

Captain Augustine Johnson, born on Saba, was a first cousin of my father. He was captain of a number of large schooners and also owned a four-masted schooner at one time, named the "Robert L. Baine." For a number of years he was the captain of the large schooner "Charles G. Endicott." He, like many of the other Saba captains, liked to have his own Saba people on his schooners with him. On the "Endicott" his crew consisted of the Mate Jeroe "Wossa" Hassell of the village of St. John's, the cook Wilson Johnson of "Booby Hill", Pietie Johnson, Thomas C. Vanterpool, Henry Johnson, and Tom Darsey as sailors, and Bloomfield Hassell as Engineer.

On this particular trip they were coming from Cadiz, Spain headed to New York with a cargo of olive oil. He had carried a load of lumber and coal from New York to Cadiz. It was winter, and everyone knows what conditions winter can bring to bear on shipping in the North Atlantic.

Halfway to New York, the large schooner sprang a leak. The crew tried desperately to bring the leak under control, but to no avail. Everyone thought that the schooner was lost. The pumps had even stopped working and could not control the amount of water pouring into the schooner. All of a sudden the pumps started working again and in a short time, everything was under control and the hold was dry. They were all wondering what could have caused the leak and what could have brought such a sudden end to it. Captain Johnson on arrival in New York decided to take the schooner to the dry dock in New York. To the amazement of all, there had been a relatively large hole, which was the obvious cause of the leak and the near disaster and loss of the schooner. The hole, however, had been filled by a fish the exact size which had been sucked in and had blocked the hole. The fish died and in its frozen condition had prevented any further leaking all the way to the dry dock in New York where their miraculous survival was revealed.

In later life Wilson Johnson, the cook, talked about the schooner. In his whole life he had seen but one schooner worth pumping out, the "Charles G. Endicott" and but one skipper so close to God that the oaths of the ship's cook fell short of the mark. He was a Saban named Augustine Johnson. "Man above men," said Wilson:

"A young God at sea, mor n' six feet, black eyes, black mustache. Seven good years I sailed on the "Endicott" with'im. Let a gale come, and he'd neither eat nor drink. Stayed on the deck all the time walkin' 'round munchin'! Watchin' the sky, watchin' the riggin'! Watchin' the men. Tidin' fore the wind in a big mouthy sea. I flops on me face in the galley. Then I crawls out to see what's up. The deck, she is ankle-deep in water. I feels' sum'thin' bumpin' me foot. Looking down I sees the skipper's head a washin' 'round like he is a dead-un. I grab 'im by the collar, pulls him outta the wet sea. A block she's broken loose above, grazed his head, knocked two spokes outta the wheel, didn't hurt the men at the wheel, but the skippers head was a sight. He open his eyes, gives me a long look and stumbles outside. Never says, how you be, where've I been or nuthin'! A few deep breaths, and pretty soon, he's walking 'round, munchin' air, watchin'.""

I could have looked at the lives of other Saba captains for this foreword. Our most well-known pirate Hiram Beakes, who is credited with coining the phrase *"Dead men tell no tales"*, would have been an interesting subject. Also my ancestor Daniel Johnson known as *"Daniel the Terror"*, or Henry Every, alias John Avery, who left some offspring on Saba would have merited some recognition. However, I chose for a captain from a period when Saba captains were well respected and made a name for themselves all over the world.

I salute Raymond for wanting to bring out this detailed history of our captains and other seamen from Saba who did us proud in former times.

Will Johnson

PREFACE

The "Iron Man" competition is well recognized for the endurance their participants must have; they must exude resilience at every moment of the specialties it entails: a 2.4 mile swim, then 112 miles on bike, and the competition ends with a full marathon (26.2 miles).

In a not so similar way, but without doubts equally challenging, a day in the life of our typical Saban ancestors is fully detailed in one of the chapters of this book.

At the end of the XVIII century (1899), Saba's population was 2,179. Over 700 of these individuals were listed on census records as mariners and able seamen, who sailed around the world on schooners and later, hundreds of them became Captains and Mates on steam ships. They spent most of the time off island navigating on the oceans of the world, either fishing or transporting precious cargo to their final destinations in many countries.

Until I was actually several years into my personal investigation, I never understood the deep calling the sea had on me. In my youth, I actually applied to become a navy cadet in my native Venezuela. Now that I have learned so much about my ancestry, I realize it was always in my genes; somehow I instinctively knew my roots were anchored deep in sea life of former times, which I had visited only once, but my heart stayed there forever. Now when I go down to the sea and visualize the arc defined by the curvature of the water in the horizon, it brings back echoes from a distant past when, as seafarers, my ancestors rode many oceans to distant worlds and back home again, challenging the sea at every wave and gust of wind.

As result of my quest to unravel the hidden past of my family, the idea of writing a book was gestating in the back of my mind even without my knowledge. As I learned more about my great-grandfather John Miller Simmons and his master carpenter abilities, the more entrenched the idea that he somehow was an active participant in the success of many Saban captains formed. To my surprise, in my visit to Saba, two of the homes he built were still standing after hundreds of years, in spite of inclement weather, hurricanes, and such. The two wooden mahogany chests he built for his traveling sons, departing to Venezuela from Curacao, both still stand strong today as a tall testimony of his honed-skills at the homes of cousins in Venezuela.

My good friend, the late Jose F. Garcia, had just finished writing his novel based on real-life characters of his family who came from the Basque country to Puerto Rico. He was my final inspiration and offered to give me some pointers.

Although I could have taken a romantic and novelistic approach, I chose to make my book as factual as possible. I have relied on Will Johnson's experience, articles and materials, genealogy websites such as FamilySearch and Ancestry.com, as well as direct contributions by family members of these men of sea via direct correspondence, and through our Facebook website "Of Saban Descent."

This book will summarize the prominent seamen from Saba; men formed in the crucible of life, hardened by apparent isolation and rugged living conditions. I will try to address not only their marine-time expertise and challenges, in which prime skills were learned in the walls of a navigation school and nurtured by seasoned captains, but also their real human nature, underpinned by strong culture and resilient morals.

As the Venezuelan saying goes: *"No son todos los que están, ni están todos los que son."* Which liberally translated means: "Not everyone made the cut and we probably missed several people." Did I leave out your ancestor? Do you have a story to tell? Please feel free to contact me at the address listed on the initial pages and I'll be happy to include their story in future editions of this book. If you have old photos of them, even better!

To all the seafaring men, and all of those who supported you on your quest, may God bless you and your descendants.

ACKNOWLEDGEMENTS

This is maybe one of the most important and difficult parts of this book because there has been so many people who have influenced the final outcome of this project, more than twenty years in the making.

My cousins **Gonzalo Garcia Simmons** and **Nelly Garcia-Bustamante,** who both asked probing questions about the purpose of the project, and helped me to clarify my own train of thought.

My late cousin **Viola Adele Simmons-Hemingway,** who opened a floodgate of information regarding my personal family tree, providing details on the siblings of my grandfather E. Stanley Simmons and their branches, mostly established in USA.

Cousins, late **Edna Louise Brown (nee Simmons), Kathleen Hands,** and **Ashley Cordi (nee Jordan),** who in their own investigations built solid documentation and preserved photographic material regarding several family members and documented family lore passed down.

Will Johnson, historian, politician, and as we would discover later in my research, a 5th Cousin as well, who with his vast experience and accumulated historic meme and supporting photographic material, has fostered many of the lines and images of this book.

My friends on our Facebook® page **"Of Saban Descent"** for all the family stories and valuable tidbits of information, helping piece the anecdotes in right order and connected to the right people. Thanks to the unselfish commitment of our co-administrators (Anne Richter, late Gösta Simmons, Henry Hassell, and Will Johnson) and the great Saban family, to educate us about Saban Lore, connecting families and their stories across distance and time.

To the late **Carl Lester Johnson,** and his sister **Bessie Kathleen Johnson-Richter** for access to their photographic material but most importantly to their meme of Saban lore.

I would like to thank those who read preliminary drafts of the text, and offered comments. These include helpful suggestions from my daughters **Karim and Stephanny Simmons,** and careful readings of the whole or major parts of the text by Lt. Colonel (Ret) Paul Calvert and Will Johnson.

Thank you to all those who have posted information on internet forums inquiring about their Saban ancestors, or authors who published books regarding Saba; the plethora of information has helped substantiate many of the stories.

In closing I want to thank **Paul McBride,** a descendant of Lieut. Commander Waldron Eugene Richard David Peter Simmons, who on July 19, 2010 made a comment regarding some photos on our Facebook page "Of Saban Descent" which stuck with me and inspired the title of this book. He commented "these were *Iron Men in Wooden Ships!*"

Finally, I celebrate the memories of many great but humble and gentle people of Saba, whom despite their challenges and tribulations have left their mark in the world and seeded our paths with their valuable lessons of life, morals and survival.

Dedication

To my father **Raymond Stanley Simmons** who passed away all too soon at the age of 66 years old, and never discovered the beautiful stories hidden in his formidable past. I know he would have enjoyed the journey.

To my mother **Emma Ortega de Simmons** and my family, who vehemently supported my passion to uncover our common roots.

To my children: **Karim Sarahi, Israel Joshua, Caroll Lee, Stephanny Ann and Raymond Stanley IV**, my inspiration and reason in life.

To my grandchildren: **Victoria Andreina, Caroline Leticia, Joshua Alejandro, Marina Isabelle** and those descendants to come, for their role in the continuation of the saga.

To all the **Families of Saban Descent**.

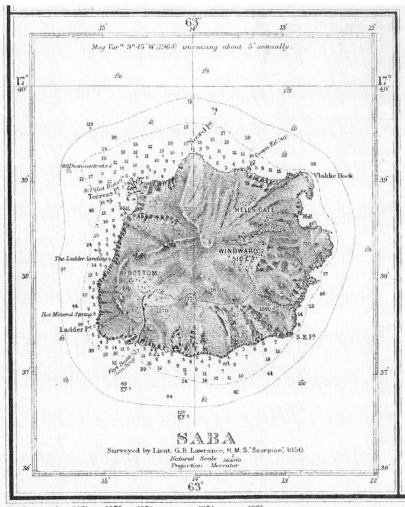

INTRODUCTION

When I first laid foot on that strange and mysterious island, I had mixed emotions, similar to the ones I felt when I walked the narrow streets of Jerusalem in the final path of Jesus Christ. There I was, about to accomplish another of my lifetime goals; another line-item off my bucket list. To walk in the footsteps of my ancestors! And, what a trip of discovery awaited me.

The first memorable moment had to be the landing of the WinAir flight on a 400 meter airstrip —the shortest commercial airport in the world– which reminded me of landing on an aircraft carrier, where at either side of the runway there is a drop into the water. Then, on to a rollercoaster-way which later I would learn was "The" road: a sinusoidal motorway that challenges any description. As I told my family later, something you have to see to believe; not even on the Swiss Alps or a Venezuelan beauty contest would you find such curves as this road going up to The Bottom, which is actually on the top!

As we drove by the quaint little houses with white wooden facades, green shutters, bright red sloping roofs and fascias (often enhanced with small gingerbread decorations), I recalled in certain way of "Colonia Tovar" in Venezuela, where a large colony of German immigrants made time stop in a deep forest in Aragua's mountains, which reminded them of home highlands and their Black Forest.

It was documented in historic chronicles that the island was first sighted by Christopher Columbus in 1493, on his second expedition to the New World and it was settled by the Dutch around 1640.

It was evident that, although we were at the end of the 20th Century, little had changed on this island despite the obvious advances of technology. Trees of mango, guava, avocado, quenepas, lime and banana lined the road; the yards well-kept not only with beautiful and colorful flowers and blooming cacti, but to my amazement also many headstones of family members long gone, but never forgotten. Once you get to know the island better, with its rugged and straight-lined volcanic terrain, you come to realize that real-estate is a very precious commodity, so Sabans make the most of whatever flat area they have at hand to build a home, a cistern, or a cemetery.

Even if it sounds incredible, Saba was almost inaccessible and way behind the rest of the world even well into early 1940's. Everything coming to or leaving Saba had to somehow overcome the challenge of the treacherous Ladder, some 800 steps cut in the rock, to come and go via Ladder Bay. As you can see from the photo below, the steepness of the steps and the abrupt change in elevation from 0 to 800 feet can really be appreciated as one reaches Ladder Bay from sea, by looking at the old customs house perched half way up. Boats could only land when the sea was calm, and even then, only by skilled and strong men who had to stand waist deep in water to handle the cargo. Everything from the outside world had to be carried up, including all sorts of cargo such as a large trunk, pianos and even a chubby bishop.

800 steps cut in the rock separate Ladder Bay from The Bottom

Elder man being transported on a human taxi – c. 1955

In old times, Sabans were able to prevent unwanted invasions defending their land from above, in a similar fashion as the inhabitants of Massada in the Dead Sea, by keeping piles of boulders stacked behind wooden supports that were cut down when attackers were half way up the hill. A road was built to Fort Bay in 1943, but with no port to shelter the bay, the island was still much impossible to reach most of the time.

We were booked at a hotel called the Captain's Quarters, which at some time had been the private home of Capt. Henry Hassell in Windwardside and had been expanded and converted into one of the finest guesthouses of the island of the time. Word had it this was Saban's favorite "water hole" and local gossip was easy to come by; just what I needed to jumpstart my investigations! I was here to learn as much as I could about my Simmons ancestry.

I had many meetings, planed and improvised, that always opened new doors and added more data, but nothing specific about my particular branch. I met with the acting Lt. Governor at the time, Will Johnson, who was a splendid host. At that juncture, Internet was in its infancy, so most of our interaction had been via FAX. Many people would greet me by name and a full "Good Morning, Mr. Simmons" looking me straight in the eyes; not just a polite and evasive "Hi". Later I would learn that the news of my arrival had already spread like bushfire from the man at the airline office Freddy Johnson, brother of my host, to many people on the island. I suppose it's hard to keep a secret in such a small island.

Mr. Johnson gave me a tour of the island and thorough explanations at each spot where we stopped: Thomas Vanterpool's home, Meggie Jane's home and even a home built by my Great grandfather, still standing over 100 years old. Later that night, we met for coffee at his home and he took me down to his library, with books all over the place, incredible stacks of randomly organize piles of paper that only he could decipher. That evening he handed me for my review a couple of folders with many copies of documents, records, and an old family bible. Back at the hotel I eagerly went through each document and made my proper annotations for my records. Written inside the bible was inscribed the full family tree of one of the Simmons families of Saba. One of the documents he handed to me was a copy of the declaration by a group of Saba citizens of their decision to honor Governor Moses Leverock for his outstanding contributions to the island by renaming the capital from "The Bottom" to "Leverocktown." At the end of the document were many signatures; there was one that shone in my eyes like the North Star: John M. Simmons, my great-grandfather!

The next day I went to visit the Cemeteries where I tried to make detailed notes of all those names that could be related. By the end of the day, I was exhausted.

Following up with me in the week, Will took me to the Government building and introduced most of the people there including Ray Hassell, whose name for some reason always stuck in my mind. Then he took me to the Census Office where the original books with vital records were kept. Ms. Marlene Sorton facilitated access to the archives, and I spent the rest of the afternoon browsing the books trying to make sense of them with my almost nonexistent Dutch. Armed with an English-Dutch dictionary facilitated by Will, I struggled to get through a few pages. As the office was about to close I made arrangements with Ms. Sorton to visit next day.

Early in the morning I had my breakfast and headed out to the Government Building. I was on a mission, ready to research my roots, and I had a feeling that this would be another great day of discoveries. My enthusiasm was met with a dark cloud, as I learned that Ms. Sorton's father had passed away that evening and the office was closed for mourning. I wrote a sympathy note with my condolences and that was it. I had to head back home.

By the time I had to leave, I was overwhelmed with so many disjointed pieces of the puzzle. I accomplished so much in my general investigation; however I was still hungry for more. In addition, as I realized when I prepared my Venezuelan roots investigation, I found there to be many people who were looking for their Saban ancestry as well. And so, was born the idea of the "Saba Family Tree" project: a non-commercial effort to help people from abroad -and sometimes even locals-, to relinquish their past and pay tribute to their ancestors. After all, it was because of their efforts and choices that I, and many of Saban descent, am now standing upon this planet.

Genealogy is an auxiliary science, which has proven helpful to many sciences: biology, medicine, history, even philosophy. However, the "Summum Bonum" of genealogy, the greater good, is connecting us to our past and helping us understand first-hand the efforts of those who came before us. My goal was simply to create a site that would serve as an important exchange and specific resource for collecting data; sharing & bartering information for those interested in piecing their Saba ancestral puzzle together.

Alex Haley, author of the famous biography of his African ancestor Kunta-Kinte, as narrated in his book "Roots", said it better than anyone: *"When an old person dies, it's like a library burning down."* Those words are driven home to anyone who has experienced the loss of a parent, grandparent or a beloved old relative. Especially, as on Saba, in a place where pillage, fire and inclement weather could destroy years of precious records, leaving us many times to guess some of the data based only on circumstantial evidence of letters, photos or family stories passed down in form a verbal meme.

"Preserving the life stories of our closest relatives is a priceless gift one generation bestows upon another" – Dorothy Shapiro

Here is a message to you my dear reader. Rather than wishing that you had somehow preserved those stories, photos, and memories, today is the day to begin the process of recording, documenting and preserving your family's history. Interview your loved ones today.

Do not be someone who later will be saying: "I wish I had asked them more about that when they were still alive"; today is your chance, and it might be the last; a stroke, a heart-attack or an accident can happen in an instant and rob us of many memories and a piece of our history. Do it now while they are here with us. Pull out the family album of old photos, get a digital recorder, and let them comment and tell the stories as they reach for the memories of your ancestors through the windows of time!

With the technology, resources, and means available to us today, this is the most tangible and everlasting way to record and preserve your family history. **Give your family the gift of heritage!**

LIFESTYLE OF SABANS

D o you think you have what it takes to live a semi-isolated life without the basic commodities which sometimes are qualified as main necessities? Would you dare to live in a place where things you take for granted in the big city have not yet come to be part of "normal life" as you conceive it (i.e. electricity, current water, cellular phones, toilets, and roads)?

That was the life and somewhat unknown magnetism of Saba. It baffles many the reasons why anyone would come (as so many did later) and actually stay on this seemingly inhospitable island. All roads, villages, buildings were built by hardworking resolute Sabans, working shoulder to shoulder in the hope that their children, someday not too far, would enjoy a better life.

The green and opulent landmass, used in the opening frames of the original 1939 version of the movie "King Kong", was portrayed at times as an "Island of Women" because families were mostly raised single-handed by strong Saban women as their husbands left for sea or in search of well-paid jobs to economically support the livelihood of their wives and children. In spite of their frail but well-formed bodies, Saba women gave special meaning to the words "strength and resolution." And yet, they did find time to paint and beautifully decorate their "gingerbread homes" with flowers, memorabilia and trinkets brought by their husbands during their trips abroad, and kept their family interred in their private plots in neatly preserved gardens or next to their homes.

Most of the inhabitants are descendants of resilient Scottish and English settlers, along with a few Africans who originally were brought as slaves. The Dutch were expelled by the pirates from Jamaica in 1665 and never returned in any great numbers. Any Dutch on Saba in later times were when a Dutch marechausee, or police officer, married a lady from Saba. The exception is that the people from "Palmetto Point" (later called Mary's Point) in 1665 took the oath of allegiance to the British and were allowed to remain on Saba. Most prominent among them was the Zeegers family, which later was spelled in a variety of ways (Zeagers/Zeagors).

The funny thing is that they always return to Saba, even if they have lived their whole lives in the United States or elsewhere.

In any event, they were forced to work alongside as they scraped a living from the rugged land; they made this land theirs by becoming mariners, fishermen, planters, cobblers and shipwrights. Saban women are well-known for their Spanish drawn thread-work, also known as "Saba Lace". Agriculture and lace-making became supplementary means of survival in addition to their husband's seafaring income; however, limited cropland had to be cleared out, by hand, of rocks and rubble to increase the arable land.

As proven by the steadfast Sabans, nothing is more powerful than the power of imagination. They were multitaskers out of necessity to help their families survive. Up until the mid-1950's, the only way to get between the villages was to walk along steep mountain footpaths. Civil engineers out of the Netherlands proclaimed that to build a road on such a rugged steep terrain was short of impossible. Sabans were unfazed by such obstacles and took this as a challenge. Josephus Lambert Hassell, a carpenter by trade born in 1906, took a correspondence course in road building and over several years the Saban people designed and hand-built their own road which connects the four main villages. It was built over the course of 25 years using only basic construction tools; no tractors nor power machines. Just picks, shovels, wheel barrels, local cement made from lava rock, and the strong determination and backbones of resolute Sabans, "heading" everything from tools, to water, to mixing the cement. It was completed in 1958, although the fist vehicle, a Jeep Willys, made its appearance in March 17th 1947.

What made Saba exceptional, and still does, is the fact that the population is an English speaking society within a Dutch colony. Dr. Hartog tried to rewrite history and make everyone and everything Dutch. Frank Hassell and Will Johnson made him change his views on "Botte", or bowl shaped, to justify the name of the capital and which the Dutch always referred to the town as "De Vallei" or The Valley.

Population clearing the field for plane landing at Flat Point

Dutch engineers were similarly disparaging about the idea of an airport. This time the Sabans called upon Rémy de Haenen, an experienced pilot from St. Barts, to evaluate the opportunity. He looked over their one and only flat-topped area on the rock, a privileged track of old sugarcane fields owned by Daniel Johnson on the east-side of the island, and figured landing might be possible. As in many occasions before, Sabans rolled-up their sleeves and worked together side by side to flatten the area as much as they could by hand, removing big rocks and filling in holes. On February 9th 1959, Rémy landed his aircraft, proving the feasibility of flying-in and taking-off the island, linking Saba to the modern world. The construction of the airport was entrusted to Jacques Deldevert and formally inaugurated on September 18th, 1963. Today Sabans have their airport, cataloged as the shortest commercial runway in the world. Flying into Saba is one of life's most interesting experiences, as exciting as landing a jet fighter on an aircraft carrier.

Aerial view of Flat Point and the construction of the airport

Still in 1963, Saba was a much different place than the contemporary "after the millennium" times in other parts of the world; Saba was behind the rest of the world by at least 40 years. There was limited running water, with cisterns to capture rain water which was drawn-out of the well with buckets on a rope. Very few households yet had the luxury of electricity and if you had the luck to be in possession of a radio or an electric iron, brought to you by a loved one from abroad, you had to be swift in using it, as the electric fluid was connected from 6:00pm to about mid-night.

On "slaughter day" one of the family members would "put off" the bull. To "put off" a bull meant that it was about to be butchered and you had to go from house to house to get people's signatures to buy a share of meat. If you had sixty people interested, the whole cow would be chopped up, divided in sixty heaps and that was your share and it was fls. 2.50 at the time. If there were only thirty people interested, the same procedure was applied and you were lucky to get a double portion for the same price.

In lieu of wax or butcher paper, fresh meat was tendered to the families neatly wrapped in clean "chinnie" or "elephant ear" leaves, which grow two or three feet in diameter. Some children would make it a point to be there the fore day to watch bull kill. Gutted and cleaned by 8:00am, distributed by 10:00am and finally cooked and eaten by 2:00pm. Out of mere necessity, and lubricated by the cold-stone fact that there was neither electric power nor refrigeration, we can say this was very efficient marketing.

Also, men would go hunt for wild goat and use every piece of the animal. The skins were cleaned, dried under a hot Caribbean sun and stretched over old nail-kegs to make drums that would be fine-tuned with heat of fire until they made the right sound. Stomach and other guts would be tossed to the pigs that greedily ate them up. Of course, the meat would be slowly cooked with different spices including curry and served with a large portion of Irish potatoes and local vegetables. Some limited families enjoyed the treat of a roasted piglet, usually reserved as a Christmas holiday indulgence.

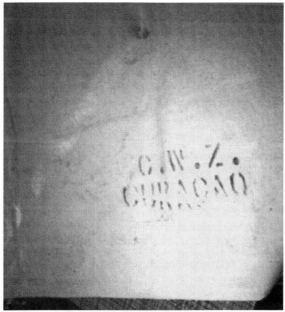

Gold Medal Flour bags used to make "sliders"

Large bags of Gold Medal Flour were imported from Carlos Winkel & Zonen (CWZ) on Curacao. People like Mrs. Helena Peterson who had a large bakery, would import many bags of flour for their treats. She would sell the empty bags to those who made clothing from them. The bags were made from a very fine-grade cotton. After the flour was used at the bakery, these bags would be thoroughly washed, and from them seamstresses would make undergarments called "sliders" and even some nice shirts, good enough to go to church with. Nothing went to waste back then.

Sometimes the women of the household would complain to the "Veldwachters" (old country constables) that when they came out to pick up their wash they were always missing underwear from the clothesline. Thinking it would be some pervert stealing, it was decided to hold a vigil on the clothesline. As it turned out, a flock of goats favored ladies underwear for their main meal of the day. Case closed!

A day in the lives of our ancestors

As a reminder to the younger generations, who probably could care less about this, the following lines cherish part of our Saba people's history.

Our elders labored very hard to make a living; got up before daybreak, milked their cow, chopped wood and put it in the kitchen under canvas covers for the lady of the house in order for it not to get wet if it rained, which would make it more difficult to ignite and burn.

The head of the household's chores involved drawing water from the cistern and filling up the pails in the kitchen so they would have it readily available for washing, cooking, etc. He would maybe make some strong coffee and eat a roasted sweet potato before leaving the house; he would take his hoe or cutlass, and a calabash nut of drinking water secured with leather straps for a day of farming. Chopping down trees, drying the wood and making charcoal for cooking, cutting grass, and moving livestock around before returning at the end of the day with a canvass bag of fresh vegetables hung on his shoulder and a large bundle of fresh cut grass for the cow in the stone pen, built from rocks with his own hands.

Cow in a stone pen on Saba

Women had many jobs besides house cleaning and hand washing clothes in a wooden tub and hanging them out to dry. They also cooked food for the pigs -mostly tania roots and green bananas- as well as the day's meals for the family.

For those households without a stone oven, to make a pastry was a big challenge; iron pot, pie in the pot on a plate, pot covered and basically twigs for fire on the cover so the top of the pie could also be baked from the top down, and look nice and brown also. Not to mention the ordeal of roasting coffee or cacao beans.

In fact, every member of the household had to perform one or more tasks, such as after school boys ran errands to the shops, the boys also had to cut grass or fetch dry wood from the mountainside or move livestock and complete the tasks the father left with mother to pass on as 'orders' to be performed.

Milking the cow by hand was one of the chores
(Thomas Eric Johnson – c. 1950)

Playtime was secondary when time permitted. Spinning homemade tops, or a game of marbles, or flying kite, were the one and only sports that popped up during the course of the year. The balls were made from stuffed old stockings. All women wore stockings. They were rolled to form a round object and wrapped with string in an effort to keep the entire mess together and sustain it for a game or two of their own version of 'cricket.' The wickets consisted of large flat rocks propped up in a standing position, and certainly, the bats were homemade as well.

Of course, the girls had chores as well, such as mending clothes, polishing the floors with hard wax and an old unused felt hat, making up beds and helping with other small children, or in the kitchen helping to cook, cleaning the house, etc. There were no toys, fingernail polish, or shampoo. Blue soap for washing clothes, a wooden tub, or galvanize bathtub sufficed for taking a bath.

Most of the young women formed part of the different church choirs and if a young woman had a sweetie or boyfriend, it was incumbent upon him to ask the head of the home permission to visit the girlfriend's home.

The men, of course, also had to find time and perform a lot of work before even considering taking-off for a day of fishing "on the rocks" or offshore on the Saba bank. It involved a double supply of grass for the cow, food for the pigs, and a good supply of wood to cook the meals while he was out having a day of fun. Moreover, what that entailed would not be something today's generation would envision.

From the Sinkhole, Upper Hells Gate, Windwardside, St. Johns or The Bottom, men would have to rise early, have breakfast, fill a large calabash water container commonly known as a "nut," (no plastic containers in those days, and a bottle of water would not suffice for a day of lots of walking and rowing and fishing), a large canvas bag with lots of cast iron sinkers, hemp fishing line, some Johnnie cakes and ripe bananas. After all the usual morning chores had been completed, they would start the long journey down to the sea shore, over hills and dales, and as arranged, meet the other four members of the boat crew. Then they moved the bank boat down to the surf, put their canvas bags in the boat, and gather a sizable amount of flat seashore smooth rocks (average each about 2 lbs maximum) oblong rocks being the choice for additional weight to send the "fit" of nine hooks and bait fast to the depths of the ocean.

Using landmarks as a guide to fish the bank and according to how they fished in those days, upon arrival to the selected spot two men in the bow end of the boat used two oars to "keep the boat on the mark." One of the fishermen would commence fishing by sending his baited hooks to the ocean floor, strikes off to get rid of the rock and wait for a bite and again strike off to set the hook in the fish and wait for hopefully more to grab the baited hooks. At some point during that time, the other three anglers baited their hooks and sent them to the ocean floor as well, before the first angler started to pull up his catch.

*As done in the old days, Saban anglers Wathey Woods, Hilton Whitfield and Heyliger
get shares of a good catch of Wahoo by a simple method of cutting, sizing and stacking.*

If it proved to be a fruitful day and a good catch, then they would return back to shore, share the fish in equal parts, cleanout and wash the inside of the boat and pull it up against the embankment. After a day of rowing, fishing, then the return trip back to the village with more weight than when they left home, but it did not end there, the fish had to be cleaned, salted and put to dry in the sun until the next day, he had to milk the cow, feed the pigs, put away his fishing gear and fill up water containers in the house if needed before he could take a bath and eat. Yes my dear reader, multitasking at its best! Using landmarks as a guide to fish the bank and according to how they fished in those days, upon arrival to the selected spot, two men in the bow end of the boat used two oars to "keep the boat on the mark." One of the fishermen would commence fishing by sending his baited hooks to the ocean floor, strikes off to get rid of the rock and wait for a bite and again strike off to set the hook in the fish and wait for hopefully more to grab the baited hooks. At some point during that time, the other three anglers baited their hooks and sent them to the ocean floor as well, before the first angler started to pull up his catch.

If it proved to be a fruitful day and a good catch, then they would return back to shore, share the fish in equal parts, and clean out and wash the inside of the boat and pull it up against the embankment. After a day of rowing, fishing, then the return trip back to the village with more weight than when they left home, but it did not end there. The fish had to be cleaned, salted and put to dry in the sun until the next day, he had to milk the cow, feed the pigs, put away his fishing gear and fill up water containers in the house if need before he could take a bath and eat.

Yes, my dear reader, there is a lesson in multitasking, survival and preservation to be learned from the history of old Saban men and women.

Capt. Frederick A. Simmons at the School of Navigation

THE NAVIGATION SCHOOL

History always has a way to developing the kind of people it needs to leave their mark. The rugged "Auld Rock" indeed stands out in the Caribbean as the cradle of captains and mariners of the Western World.

The character of the people of Saba, included qualities of toughness, endurance, seamanship and maritime enterprise, which sprang from the peculiar amphibious and isolated nature of the island, and which differs from that of any other islands in that there was no natural port or beaches.

Although Saba and its men had already gained well deserved fame with their experience and maritime knowledge, the spark that initiated Saba's future in the sea could have been reinforced by the socialist member of the Lower Chamber, Henri van Kol (1852-1925), who traveled to the Antilles on his own initiative and published his findings in a travel report full of critical remarks. In loud voice he cried "shame on The Netherlands for the neglect of their islands." Besides recommending that the Saba's population be moved to Sint Eustatius to plant potatoes there, he also recommended imparting lessons in navigation to the population. (Kol, 1904). In 1907 a book was published containing a research on fisheries in the islands then known as "Curaçao and dependencies." At that time, Dr. Julius Herman Boeke had also echoed these same concerns after his trip in 1905.

In 1907, the Minister in charge was finally convinced that a navigation school would be a good thing for the island. He approved some money on the budget as well as instructions as to how the school should be run.

Capt. Frederick Augustus Simmons was given permission in 1909 to start the school and he did so for thirteen years until he became ill and died. At this location he educated embryo sailor-men, still in their knickerbockers, in the use of the tools of the trade - sextant and chronometer-, to find their way in the sea amongst the stars.

The navigation school was centered on wooden sail ships (mostly schooners) and rowboats but the solid principals, discipline and navigation skills learned there became the cornerstone for the young mariners' life. The men that studied navigation here made their way to the mainstream shipping routes such as United States, and went on to sturdy steamships and left their mark in the world, mostly as merchant mariners but also showed great valor in times of war. As before the schooners, - which had displaced the square-rigged ships in commercial routes because of their speed, agility and less manpower required-, despite their efficiency, steamships drove the schooners away from the seas with their speed and large cargo capacity.

This school produced around 150 licensed captains during the years it existed. They left on to New York, received further training and went on to become captains of clipper ships, steamships and even cruise ships. The stern living conditions on the island forced the families to plan ahead and be organized in everything they did, from working their lands, setting up agriculture, raising cows & goats for milk, meat and manure, to their shipping skills.

Embryo sailor-men still in their short trousers, learned to use the tools
of men of the trade to find their way in the sea amongst the stars.

This organized life-style was fundamental in the basic sailing skills, developed out of need by many Sabans. By quintessential need, a sailing vessel must be the perfect model of order and systems reflected in the best practice of seafaring traditions. Order and organization are foremost instrumental in the success of a sail ship. The rigging, masting and fitting-out of a sail ship is a great task but yet again, a small undertaking when compared to the work of care and maintenance required for each rope, spar, and sail.

Frederick A. Simmons was the official instructor appointed by the government; however Capt. Arthur Wallace Simmons (the son of Richard Simmons and Peter Ann Darsey) and his son Capt. Edward Rudolph Simmons would lend a hand to fill-in and impart the class with their own knowledge and proven skills when Freddie was on sick leave, or away on business. Students came to the navigation school mostly from Windwardside, St. John's and The Bottom as well.

Despite the power and speed of steamships, sail ships never really disappeared. The largest wooden vessels to hold out longest were the clippers, transporting grain from Australia to Europe up to WW II. The Dutch schooner "Blue Peter" plied the route of the Caribbean Windward Island - Leeward Islands in the Netherlands Antilles until well after 1950- and many schooners were used along the coast of America and the Caribbean inter-island trade.

A roll-list of students of Windwardside registered in the Saba Navigation School – January 1920

Type of Ships

Most seafaring Sabans had an early start in their love of sea and ships at a young age. As early as their thirteenth birthday, still using short trousers, many were appointed as "Cabin Boys" with no pay, just board and room, and the real life opportunity to put in practice the knowledge learned at school. After two years, the captain of the ship would gladly issue a letter of recommendation which would attest to their gained skills and strengths, and open the doors to a whole new world.

These are some of the type of ships they navigated, including the fishermen's rowboats which would visit the rich Saba Bank to harvest grouper, sailfish, wahoo and occasional lobsters and sea turtles.

Row Boats

Between 1629 and 1972 all landings on Saba, whether people or cargo, took place at the Fort Bay and to a lesser extent at the Ladder Bay using sturdy rowboats. These lighter boats would be built from heavy cedar ribs from trees on Saba's Mount Scenery and sometimes even the planks were made from the wood of the cedar tree.

Putting their backs into it!

Sloop

A sloop (from Dutch sleep) is a sail boat with a fore-and-aft rig and a single mast farther forward than the mast of a cutter. A sloop's fore-triangle is smaller than a cutter's, and unlike a cutter, a sloop usually bends only one headsail, though this distinction is not definitive; some sloops have more than one. Ultimately, the position of the mast in the first third of the ship is the most important factor in determining whether a ship is considered as a sloop

Sloops heading out to sea.

On a gaff rigged, single-masted boat, the clearest distinction between a sloop and a cutter is the run of the forestay. On the sloop, it runs to the outboard end of the bowsprit, which means that the bowsprit must always stay in position and cannot be retracted. On a cutter, the forestay runs to the stem head of the hull. This allows the bowsprit to be run back inboard and stowed. This can be helpful in crowded harbors or when stowing the jib in strong wind conditions. (University)

Yawl

A yawl (from Dutch Jol) is a two-masted sailing craft similar to a sloop or cutter but with an additional mast (mizzenmast or mizzen mast) located well aft of the main mast, often right on the transom, specifically aft of the rudderpost (a vessel with the mizzenmast located forward of the rudderpost is called a ketch). A mizzen sail (smaller than the mainsail) is hoisted on the mizzenmast.

In its heyday, the rig was particularly popular with single-handed sailors; this was due to the ability of a yawl to be trimmed to sail without rudder input. (University)

Schooner

A schooner is a type of sailing vessel characterized by the use of fore-and-aft sails on two or more masts with the forward mast being no taller than the rear masts. Schooners were first used by the Dutch in the XVI or XVII century.

Two-masted schooners were and are most common. They were popular in trades that required speed and windward ability, such as slaving, privateering, blockade running.

Two-masted schooners were and are most common.

Legend has it that during the first launch of this type of ship built by Andrew Robinson, a spectator exclaimed "Oh, look how she scoons", scoon being similar to scon, a Scots word meaning to 'skip along the surface of the water'. Andrew Robinson is quoted of coining the term, "A schooner let her be."

The four-masted schooners attempted to reduce individual sail area, increase net tonnage to reach 500 to 700 tons. They were still able to manage with a relatively small crew of eight hands. Sails, originally hoisted in early days by hand, were gradually improved with the gasoline-hoisting engines bringing savings in work, wages, and food.

The largest wooden schooner ever built was the 'Wyoming', six-masted, whose registered length was 329.5 feet, but her length from the tip of the jibboom to the taffrail (stern rail) was 426 feet; she was capable of carrying 6600 tons (6000 long tons) of coal. Despite its size, the Wyoming could be handled by a crew of only eleven to fourteen men. The normal crew consisted of eight sailors, two mates, a cook, an engineer and a captain; that was all the manpower needed to manage the colossal vessel.

She was officially launched on December 15, 1909 at the Percy and Small shipyard in Bath, Maine. After approximately 25 years in service, a terrible winter storm destroyed the Wyoming and her entire crew on March 11, 1924, in the vicinity of Pollock Rip Channel between Martha's Vineyard and Cape Cod (University). From interviews held with Capt. Irvin Holm, by Will Johnson, we learned that some Sabans sailed on her: Capt. Irvin Holm (Mate) and Ralph Hassell (Donkeyman), as well as sailors Simon Hassell and Edward Peterson.

The loss of the Wyoming accelerated the demise of the era of the great schooners, with no new ones being built after WW I. Schooners we already loosing space to the coal barges and the steam colliers with huge economic and technological advantages.

By the way, the Book of Genesis says that Noah's Ark was 300 cubits long. That comes to the same length as the Wyoming (make of it what you may.)

Liberty Ships

Upon seeing the design for the Liberty ship, which was based on a British ship first built in 1879, President Roosevelt named her "the ugly duckling."

The Liberty ships were designed and built to a standardized, mass produced style as never seen before. The 250,000 parts were pre-fabricated all over the country and the 250-ton sections, complete with portholes and mirrors, were miraculously welded together in as little as four and a half days. A full-fledged Liberty ship cost under $2,000,000.

The Liberty (officially an EC2) was 441 feet long and 56 feet wide. Her three-cylinder, reciprocating steam engine, fed by two oil-burning boilers produced 2,500hp and a speed of 11 knots. Her five holds could carry over 9,000 tons of cargo, plus airplanes, tanks, and locomotives lashed to its deck. A Liberty could carry 2,840 jeeps, 440 tanks, or 230 million rounds of rifle ammunition.

Liberty ships carried a crew of about 44 seamen, and 12 to 25 Naval Armed Guards. Some Liberty Ships were also armed with:

- One 4 inch stern gun
- Two 37 mm bow guns
- Six 20 mm machine guns

Liberty ship USS Alanthus a wooden World War I commanded by Capt. Ernest Alfred Johnson

Many technological advances were made during the Liberty shipbuilding program in WW II. A steel cold-rolling process was developed to save steel in the making of lightweight cargo booms. Welding techniques also advanced sufficiently to produce the first all-welded ships. Prefabrication was perfected, with complete deckhouses, double-bottom sections, stern-frame assemblies and bow units speeding production of the ships. By 1944, the average time to build a ship was 42 days. In all, 2,751 Liberties were built between 1941 and 1945, making them the largest class of ships built worldwide.

These new and improved Liberty ships carried a crew of between 38 and 62 civilian merchant sailors, and 21 to 40 naval personnel to operate defensive guns and communications equipment. The Merchant Marine served in World War II as a Military Auxiliary. Of the nearly quarter million volunteer merchant mariners who served during World War II, over 9,000 died. Merchant sailors suffered a greater percentage of fatalities (3.9%) than any branch of the armed forces.

About 200 Liberty ships were lost to torpedoes, mines, explosions, kamikazes, etc., during WWII.

Tankers

Tankers were developed around the turn of the century to carry liquid cargo: gasoline, oil, or molasses. During World War II, American tankers made 6,500 voyages to carry 65 million tons of oil and gasoline from the U.S. and the Caribbean to the war zones and to the Allied forces. They supplied 80% of the fuel used by bombers, tanks, jeeps and ships during the War and also transported troops, ammunition and spare parts. Sabans commanded many of these tankers, and many had crew members from there as well.

SS Mielero one unique designed ship capable of transporting both oil and molasses without having to change tanks.

The Second World War ended the era of the great fishing schooners. Replaced by modern steel trawlers, the fleets of sailing salt-bankers no longer set out to challenge the cruel North Atlantic to reap a harvest of cod for the markets of the world. Nevertheless, schooners remained dominant in the coastal trade.

OUR SABAN ORIGINS

A s George W. Prothero wisely stated: *"The roots of the present lie deep in the past;* and the real significance of contemporary events cannot be grasped unless the historical causes which have led to them are known."

Unfortunately hurricanes in 1772, 1780 and 1787, fires and invasions have destroyed and erased many valuable records one would usually use to study history of Saba. As Frederic A. Fenger stated in his book *Alone in the Caribbean*: "What ancient documents Saba may have possessed were whisked up and blown out across the wide seas over a century ago when a hurricane swept the island in 1787 and took with it almost every vestige of human habitation except the low–set concrete covered rain tanks and the tombs of the ancestors of the present inhabitants." On the other hand, high level of illiteracy and poor record keeping of the time has created a "blurred vision" to the past. My personal sense on the Saban origins is that when Henry Morgan came and established himself in Jamaica, from where he controlled the rest of England's interests in the Caribbean, he "seeded" the islands with his men and their families to ensure control and loyalty. But before that, we know the island of Saba was handed over or taken by other states as well.

The British influence is not only evident in their beautiful accents which a professional linguist could probably place to a specific region in Europe, but also by the fact that English language has been preserved deep in the island's roots regardless of the passing of control from France, England, Sweden, Spain and The Netherlands.

Dutch historians have constantly tried to make the native islanders as descended of Dutch settlers. Even new arrogant neo-colonialists tell people that Sabans never contributed anything to their own history and that we are telling history in our own way without proper research and so on.

As a gift to Will Johnson, Ryan Espersen (MPhil, MA - Archaeology from Leiden, Netherlands) retrieved the Burgher list for the year 1823 on Saba

Island directly from the archives in The Hague. The surnames listed there are *Beaks, Beal, Collins, Darsey, Davis, Dinzey, Every, Hassell, Horton, Johnson, Keeve, Leverock, Mardenborough, Peterson, Simmons, Winfield and Zeagors*. These residents of 1823 can trace their ancestry back to 1665 when pirates from Jamaica captured the island. Others go back to settlers from St. Kitts from 1629. They naysayers should check this population list of 1823 and tell us who is a Dutchman on the list.

When Charles Herbert of National Geographic came to Saba in November 1940, one of his assistants asked; "Where did these people come from?" Mr. Herbert answered, "They are from Scotland and their accent is Broad Scots Lowland." The way to identify it is by the way many old timers speak: "Look he's a'falling," "He's a'walking," "He's a'drinking water." The old Sabans like my great-grandparents hardly ever said 'yes'. It was always 'aye'. Also, every valley on Saba is referred to as a Ghaut, which comes from old Scottish too. Although we are of Anglo/Gaelic beginnings Saba was separated from the cultural mores of those beginnings for so long that Sabans became people with their own culture, in which they retained the desire for education and intellectual prowess, similar to the Scotts. My cousin Caroline M. Myrick and her colleague spent a few weeks on Saba and did a study on *"What is Saban English?: A Sociolinguistic Analysis of a Caribbean Dialect Isolate."* Thanks to her excellent work she was accepted in the Sociology/linguistics PHD program at North Carolina State University, and was offered a full scholarship.

Without going so deep into linguistics, it is fairly easy to identify physical profiles of traits of all these races in the fair skin redheads, blonds, blue/green eye Sabans. Also colored people, who probably came from slave plantations in the Caribbean, most likely have their roots in the African continent.

The 1823 Population List provides information that goes beyond my "gut feeling" that this is the origin of my Simmons branch; I think that a thorough DNA study of Saba's inhabitants could show important migration patterns which when contrasted to history records could tell us a thing or two about the real origins of Saban folks.

I have tried to layout the timetable of events as they have been documented by several sources, and as I understand them, which were instrumental in the foundation of *"The Auld Rock"*.

1500's

It was Juan De La Cosa, - called the most expert mariner and pilot of his age -, who accompanied Columbus on his second voyage and who, in the year 1500, executed a map known as 'A Portolan Chart of the World'.

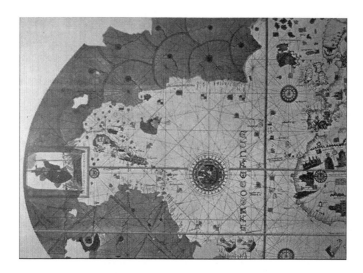

Portolan Chart of the World by Juan de la Cosa

It is this map of De La Cosa, -which may or may not have been patterned after Cabot's World map-, which shows the island of Saba for the very first time in the annals of history.

This may close the first milestone in Saba's earlier life, as far as our historical knowledge goes. If at that time there were people living there some authors believe they were Carib or Arawak Indians; others point to an extinct aboriginal race. Whoever they were, the one fact definitely remains that since Columbus' time no Conquistador ever set foot on or approached the then considered barren rock, even within a few miles.

1600's

Netherlands becomes independent from Spain in 1609 and signs a twelve-year truce (Truce of Antwerp) to finish the Eighty Years War.

Spanish domination of the seas is quite evident, transporting goods and precious metals from the Americas and the Caribbean. Saba is claimed several times with little or no settlements by the English, French, Spaniards, and Dutch.

In 1632 a group of shipwrecked Englishmen landed upon Saba; they stated they found the island uninhabited when they were rescued by others. But there has been some archeological evidence found indicating that Carib or Arawak Indians may have been on the island. In 1635 a stray Frenchman claimed Saba for Louis XIII of France

1621

The Dutch West India Company was a corporation of Dutch merchants. Among its founding fathers was Willem Usselincx (1567-1647?). The Republic of the Seven United Netherlands granted a charter on June 3, 1621, for a commercial trade monopoly in the West Indies (meaning the Caribbean), and given jurisdiction over the African slave trade in Brazil, the Caribbean, and North America.

The company was initially relatively successful; between the 1620s and 1630s, most of the Dutch trade posts or colonies were established. The New Netherlands area, which included New Amsterdam, covered parts of present-day New York, Connecticut, Delaware, and New Jersey. Other settlements were established on the Netherlands Antilles, several other Caribbean islands, Suriname and Guyana.

The largest success for the DWIC in its history was the seizure of the Spanish silver fleet, which carried silver from Spanish colonies to Spain by Pieter Pietersen Heyn in 1628; privateering, and not colonizing, was at first the objective and the most profitable activity for the Caribbean Sea.

It is very likely that the Zeeland patroon colony on Sint Eustatius occupied Saba by sending a group of colonists with orders to establish a permanent settlement on the island. Initially the DWIC disputed the rights of the Zeeland patroons to do this, but since they could prove their title, they were recognized by the DWIC as the owners.

Immigration was promoted by the DWIC, who used the patroon system to incentive settlers to come. The Patroon was a landholder with manorial rights to large tracts of land to be developed over four years and 50 families.

As result of the 1629 'Charter of Freedoms & Exception' the Dutch grant this 'Title & Land' privileges to some of the investors. The settlers of three Dutch Windward islands came from Zeeland, but at the same time were being joined by evacuated sugar planters from the recently lost sugar plantations in Brazil, seamen and soldiers left behind by ships, as well as French & Englishmen from neighboring islands.

The merchants from Zeeland that obtained charter from the DWIC, initially set up bases on:

- Tobago (1628)
- St. Maarten (1632)
- Sint Eustatius (1636)
- Saba (1640)

Saba's destiny was always tied to Sint Eustatius, only seventeen miles away. Back in the days of the pirates, times were rather simple. The biggest problem was staying alive, however the island often remained "undisturbed" while surrounding islands were attacked, pillaged, and plundered.

In 1665 when the Morgan brothers Edward and Thomas, -uncles of Sir Henry Morgan- captured Saba, there were already a good number of English, Irish and Scottish people living there. Thomas Morgan was established as the Commander of Saba, and evicted the DWIC Dutch settlers to the English colonies and let the others remain. This is one of the few times that the rough terrain of Saba was successfully invaded.

About the same time, around 90 of their English pirates defected and remained on Saba. This entire mixed group, from 1665 onward, formed the basis of the future population.

Between 1665 and 1667, while the Dutch and England were at war, Jamaican Governor Modyford assembled buccaneers to attack the Dutch islands in the Caribbean.

Henry Morgan became the terror of all Spaniards in the West Indies. By 1668, he was already an English vice-admiral of a large fleet of ships and at the same time, the pirates elected him successor to Edward Mansfield (leader of all pirate activities based in Jamaica).

After the death of Henry Morgan's uncle Edward in the late 1660s (who had been Lt. Governor after the restoration of the monarchy and whose daughter, Mary Elizabeth, Morgan would eventually marry), Governor Modyford had no reservations in naming Morgan commander of the militia in Port Royal.

In 1679, the successors of the original patroons sold half of their rights to Sint Eustatius and Saba to the DWIC. In 1683, they sold the other half to the Company as well. As with Sint Eustatius, throughout history the island of Saba changed hands nearly 20 times between the French, English, and Dutch.

Still under Dutch domain, one can see the population lists of 1699 were flawed. Obviously written by some Dutch official with poor understanding of the English language, they wrote down the names the way they phonetically sounded in Dutch. For instance, Charles Simmons became Sharles Sijmonz, Peterson as Pietersen, Blyden as Blijden, Heyliger as Heijliger and so on, which adds difficulty when trying to research these names and origins.

1700's

However, looking at the 1705 population lists (just six years later) these same inhabitants have their proper English names written, and the handwriting on the census records tells you that an intelligent schooled person wrote down the names. As a matter of fact, certain surnames such as 'van der Poole' have been Anglicized to Vanterpool.

1800's and after

The Netherlands finally took over in 1816, and that is how it remains today.

Most notably, pirate Hiriam Beakes - a nephew of Governor Edward Beaks Jr.- who coined the phrase *"Dead Men Tell No Tales"* took residence on Saba. Sugar and rum were Saba's chief exports through the 18th century, as well as fishing (particularly lobster fishing) later. Once trade routes became more open, 'Saba Lace' (a derivative of Spanish drawn thread) became very popular. By 1928, the women of Saba were exporting US $15,000 worth of lace yearly (almost $195,000 in 2014 figures).

For a long time the only way in and out of Saba was through treacherous Fort Bay and the Ladder. Geologically, the island of Saba owes its appearance above the water level to a fold in the sea crust. It is a tiny speck in the midst of that great chain of islands, extending from the coast of Florida to the northeast shores of South America, that lies almost astride what we are in the habit of calling the Trade Routes to the Panama Canal and enclosing, or encompassing, the Caribbean Sea.

Saba and the rest of these islands in the Leeward-Windward chain may have been the summits of the Caribbean Andes, that mighty range of mountains and hills which in a very distant age may have united the Americas but of which parts may have been submerged by a cataclysm as violent as nature has ever experienced, and which allowed others to remain standing with their cones just above the ocean. Saba is one of those cones as are the rest of the islands in the Leeward and Windward group.

A mere five miles in diameter, Saba rises from the sea to 3,000 feet as the highest landmark of the Netherlands Kingdom, and looks like an image in a child's fairy tale illustration. You see tall vertical cliffs of red, pink, and brown, and high in the hills, you will find houses perched in seemingly impossible positions at the edge of precipices.

As part of the Netherlands Antilles, Saba gained partial independence from The Netherlands in 1954. The issue of the Antilles' constitutional status never left the political agenda, however, and was the subject of a referendum on the three Windward Islands in 1994. All three voted to remain within the Antilles but Saba registered the largest majority of 91 per cent.

After the dissolution of the Netherlands Antilles in 2010, Saba became on October 19, 2010 a special municipality of The Netherlands and is under the direct administration of the European country.

The following is a list of people mostly native to the island. There are some included in the list that have either lived on the island for most of their adult life, or have made a significant contributions to the welfare of the island through their personal endeavors.

- Hiram Beakes, pirate
- Atthelo Edwards, introduced electric lights to Saba
- Joseph Lambert Hassell, "The Road" engineer
- Lisa Hassell, cultural foundation president
- Peter Elenor Hassell, bush medicine practitioner
- Ann Elizabeth Johnson, bush medicine practitioner
- Edwin J. Hill, Recipient (posthumously) of the United States Navy Medal of Honor for heroism during the Japanese attack on Pearl Harbor
- Chris Johnson, island council member
- Freddy Johnson, aviation pioneer
- Jonathan Johnson, Lt. Governor
- Mary Gertrude Hassell Johnson, introduced lacework industry in Saba
- Patricia Johnson, artist
- Sandra Johnson, artist, poet
- Will Johnson, historian, politician
- Cornelia R. Jones (Cutchie), first female council member
- Barbara Every Kassab, artist
- Akilah Levenstone, island council member
- Elmer Linzey, introduced electric lights to Saba
- Rufus Linzey, introduced electric lights to Saba
- Angelita Peterson, artist
- Joseph Richardson, former administrator
- Stella Richardson-Sloterdijk, poet
- Stacey Simmons, artist
- Rolando Wilson, island council member
- Bruce Zagers, commissioner of finance

SHIP BUILDING ON SABA

y great-grandfather, John Miller Simmons, was a Master
Carpenter who as many Sabans would built ships, by
rudimentary but proven methods and measurements passed
down by his teachers in the trade. He was an exceptional
woodcrafter and put special care in his family projects.

John Miller Simmons, Master Carpenter

In mid 1890s, he built two mahogany chests for his sons who were setting
off to Venezuela. These beautiful works of art still survive nowadays as
gifts within this particular branch of Simmons descendants in Venezuela.
The trunk built for my granduncle Raymond Miller Simmons is in the
hands of Cousin Nelly Bustamante (nee Garcia) and the other
corresponding to my grandfather Eugene Stanley Simmons is at the home
of Gloria Garcia, both given as gifts by my Aunt Haydee Rincon (nee
Simmons). These fabulous pieces come to show the artful and intricate
work of John Miller Simmons. With many dovetail joined drawers, brass

fittings and hidden secret compartments, these trunks are living proof of his mastery of boat building.

To build your own vessel, either a schooner or large rowboat, on Saba in those times was nothing short of remarkable. First of all, the selection, collection, retrieval and treatment of the wood alone were an amazing feat. These lighter boats would be built from heavy cedar ribs from trees here on Saba and sometimes even the planks were made from the wood of the cedar tree. In former times people from Anguilla and other islands would come to Saba to cut timber such as cedar for making their boats. It was easier to work with it than other hard woods.

Each vessel, whether powered by man, machine or wind, needs precise dimensions and characteristics to make sure it would perform as expected, or better yet, especially when pressed for need. Whether a round broad-bottom boat coaster, appropriate for hauling cargo to and from anchored ships, or schooners that would take full advantage of the lightest breeze when her canvas was spread high and wide, to safely transport passengers and cargo; each model carried it secrets.

With no power source available, regardless of the model, the size of the ship multiplied the painstaking job of using rudimentary tools such as saws, axes, smoothing planes, chisels, lap clamps, braces and bits, spoke shaves, and adzes made it no easy task to build a solid ship; it took considerable time to build a boat, and then physically hand-carry the heavy structure made from heavy 3/4" spruce planking and cedar ribs, over hill and dale, and many steps down to the Fort Bay without doing any damage to the vessel.

Setting up the frames, transom and stern, and traditional wooden lapstrakes clench, nailing would provide the planks the tight seal. Building in lapstrake is a fine art and mostly a lost one these days except in a few specialized boat centers around the world. At the stem and transom, where the planks come together, the strakes need expert treatment and call for fine woodworking skills.

Island treasurer, postmaster and shipwright Kenneth Peterson building a row boat

Older wooden boats without caulking would open cracks along the seams if they dried out for too long, but when allowed to soak in water again for a couple of days, the wood would swell and cure that problem with a tight seal. Nowadays, a fine bead of polyurethane would make it easier to form a watertight seal along the plank edges but, in the times of my great grandfather, it was the skill of the shipwright alone that kept the water out and the ships afloat.

It was with a sense of great pride that John William "Willie" Johnson told Will Johnson the story of how these schooners were built. The same goes for Harry L. Johnson who did a lot of research on the subject and also as a boy sailed on some of these schooners.

John Miller Simmons was well respected in the community of The Bottom, and also had a great friendship and was well trusted by Frederick Augustus Simmons, as reflected in certain property records where Frederick appoints John Miller Simmons as his Attorney to represent him in several property transactions when he was temporary living in Grenada.

AFSCHRIFT. *aan OnderGeull Saba*

CONSULATE FOR THE NETHERLANDS,
BARBADOS, B . W . I .

_ *1.813*

BRIDGETOWN, 21st August 1942

Ingekomen
7 Sep. 1942
1559

20/9/42
504

No. 22.

Sir,

I have the honour to advise that, by Bill of Sale
signed before me yesterday, the Netherlands Schooner " ESTER
ANITA", registered at Saba under No. 7, 17th October 1924
has been transformed from David Hassell to Thomas Charles
Barnes, a Netherlands Subject, residing at St. Barths.

The vessel was sold for the sum of $ 10,000, British
West Indian Currency.

The new owner will in due time present the document
for registration.

I have the honour to be,

Sir,

Your obedient servant,

w.g. Onleesbaar

Consul.

THE HON: THE ADMINISTRATOR
GOVERNMENT OF ST. MARTIN.
ST. MARTIN . N. W. I.

Voor eensluidend afschrift
De Gezaghebber,

Bill of Sale of the Schooner "Esther Anita"

PURCHASING THEIR WAY ON TO THE HIGH SEAS

The limitations of not having a proper dry-dock forced many captains to seek larger vessels abroad. Large schooners were purchased in the Rhode Island or Massachusetts, United States, St. Thomas and Barbados to pursue the Caribbean trade and also carry passengers who were seeking jobs in the Panama Canal construction, and the oil refineries of Aruba and Curacao. This trade route in particular became very profitable, and the owners of these schooners increase their wealth with these routes. Two notable names in this category are Capt. Abraham Benjamin Hassell and Thomas Charles Vanterpool.

In 1906 Capt. Hassell bought the schooner "Frolic" which had been impounded by the government for illegal use in transporting Chinese from Cuba to this country. He sold the "Frolic" in French Guiana at a handsome profit and started his business of purchasing and selling schooners.

For the next quarter century he bought various schooners, which he had repaired and refitted at Gloucester, Mass., reselling them in Puerto Rico, Barbados and the Virgin Islands. One of the crafts he sold was the schooner "Virginia", built at the Herreshoff shipyard in Bristol, which was used for delivering mail to Saba.

The following is a partial list of many transactions for the purchase of sloops and schooners between 1860 and 1940 or so, owned by Saban captains. Many of them were bought in Gloucester, Mass. or in Nova Scotia.

We, the undersigned John Simmons and Phoenix Simmons, ship carpenters in this island Saba, do hereby certify and declare that we were employed by His Honor Moses Leverock to assist at the building of the schooner "Harbinger" in this island in the year 1861, and we further certify and declare that the master carpenter who conducted in the building of said schooner is now dead. Saba 22nd September 1871.

I, the undersigned Moses Leverock do hereby certify and declare that the above mentioned schooner "Harbinger" is owned jointly with me by my brother Captain John William Leverock and my nephews Moses Leverock Simmons and James Simmons and my niece Ann Simmons, in the proportion of one eighth by each of them, the remaining half self. Saba 22nd December 1871.

We, the undersigned Moses Leverock, John William Leverock, and Moses Leverock Simmons, residing in this island of Saba, do hereby certify and declare: that the schooner named "Harbinger", having one deck and two masts, measuring forty-eight sea tons and commanded by John William Leverock, belongs partly to us in the following proportions: viz. Moses Leverock one half; John William Leverock, one eighth; Moses Leverock Simmons, one eight; that the other two eights belong to James Simmons and Ann Simmons; that we are Dutch burgers, natives of this island of Saba; that the administration of all that concerns said schooner "Harbinger" is conducted in this island of Saba; and that neither by our free will nor consent shall our vessel ever be put on a war footing in opposition to the authorities of the State or of the Colonies. Saba 23rd December 1871.

The above declaration has been compared by me with the certificate of tonnage and proof of property, which documents I have found conformable to the above declaration, and it results by the examination of those pieces, that the said vessel answers to the requirements stipulated by Article 2nd of the Royal Decree of the 28th May 1871 No 18 published in the colony by decree 10/12 July 1871, Publication No. 12. The declaration found in form in the presence of the recording Secretary has been affirmed by His Honor Moses Leverock, Capt. John William Leverock and Mr. Moses Leverock Simmons, residing in this island of Saba, and confirmed before me under oath, according to the religious creed of the declarers. Saba, 23rd December 1871. Substitute Canton Judge William Mitchell. Recording Secretary H. Hassell.

The 'Harbinger' was sold in 1890 in Colombia and renamed the 'Segunda Maria'. As late as 1930 she was seen in Curacao by Capt. Randolf Dunkin, loading goods for Colombia.

Captain Tommy Vanterpool who owned the home which is now the residence of the Lt. Governor owned a large number of schooners in his lifetime. The largest was the 'Mayflower' which was 147 feet long and weighed 190.27 tons. This schooner was built in Gloucester, Mass., to compete in the "Bluenose" races.

The 'Ina Vanterpool', 105 feet long and 191.30 tons was lost off Sint Eustatius on September 16th, 1926. Captain Tommy paid f.162.500 for this three master schooner. She was built by Captain Lovelock Hassell in Jamestown, Barbados and could carry 100 tons of cargo. Besides carrying freight and passengers, Captain Tommy also had the contract to carry the mail between the Northern Dutch islands and Curacao.

Mullet Bay, Barbados contains a singular graveyard. Not a graveyard in the traditional sense of the word, but as a collection of skeletons of many sunken ships. Some vessels that were claimed by Mullet Bay include the *St. Jarnan,* and two American schooners, the two-masted *Priscilla* and the four-masted *Sally Wren.* The schooner *Priscilla,* owned by Capt. Thomas Charles Vanterpool, was one of the largest boats in the Newport Bermuda Yacht Race of 1907. After a single voyage to the Turks and Caicos Islands carrying salt, *Priscilla* returned to Bermuda and sprang a plank in 1911. The vessel's ribs remain to this day.

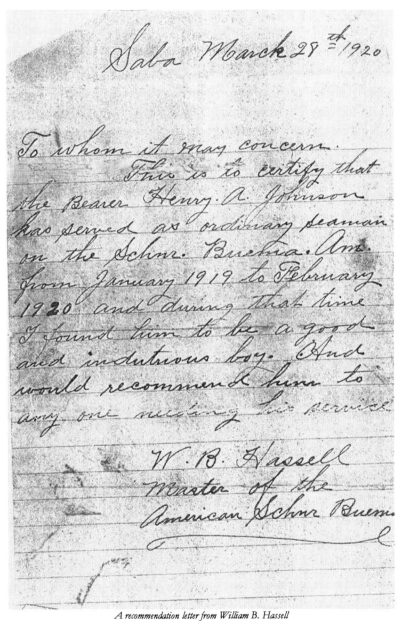

A recommendation letter from William B. Hassell

An Angel Called Kaliski

O ne freezing winter night the *"SS Caracas"* had arrived to New York City. Among the seasoned seamen was young sailor, still finding his way around in the big city. With bitter cold cutting through his skin, -so chilly that the saliva would freeze in his mouth-, he started walking the streets. With only $4 in his pockets and nowhere to go, he had to wait until next day to collect his pay!

"Do you need help, mister?" asked a man who was walking down the street toward him. *"I could certainly use some,"* he responded.

And that's how the young seaman, - Stanley Isadore Johnson-, like many other Sabans before him, met an "angel" called Hyman 'Herman' Kaliski, a Jewish merchant of German ancestry who befriended many of the Sabans who roamed the seas or came to USA via New York. Mr. Kaliski's shop at 27 South St. in South Port, New York became home away from home for many Sabans.

Hyman Kaliski's shop with the awning at 27 South St. in South Port, New York

In former times when a boy graduated from the Saba School of Navigation or completed his apprenticeship aboard a sailing vessel he was sent to Mr. Kaliski, usually with a note or recommendation. If he was from "well to do" parents he would continue his navigation studies in New York and go on as Mates and Master Mariners on the steamships. In all other cases Kaliski would suit him out with a year's worth of clothing and other seaman's gear, find him a schooner or vessel and have him shipped out to China or wherever the ship would be bound to. Kaliski served not only as a clothier, but as a banker, a post office, a social gathering place where the Saban sailors could meet and relax. We can even find evidence of him being a character witness on many Saban's naturalization paperwork. He did not allow any drinking in his place but next door was Mr. Baum's rum shop which was quite convenient. He was so popular with the Saba people for almost 40 years that some people on Saba added his name to their children. We know of at least one 'John Kaliski Jackson' who died in 1925 at the young age of twelve, but there were also one or two others born in New York of Saban descent.

Mr. Hyman Kalinski, photo courtesy of one of his Great Grand-daughters.

During his many years of honest dealings with Saba people there are a number of transactions recorded in the registers on Saba mentioning his role of which we will only mention two:

> *Power-of-Attorney to Herman Kaliski residing New York City from Henrietta Johnson residing Windwardside to collect $1,000.-- due to her by the order of the Maccabees. Saba, March 7th, 1919.*

> *Power-of-Attorney; Annie Peterson born Hassell residing Windwardside empowers Herman Kaliski resident of twenty-seven South Street N.Y.C. to collect monies left her by her deceased husband Edward Beaks Peterson (lost at sea). Saba, May 7th, 1920.*

Many sailors and captains from Saba who were lost at sea had savings in the Seaman's Bank in New York just a few blocks away from Pier 17, or life insurance, back wages and so on. Mr. Kaliski took care of all these matters for the families on Saba, and did so free of charge.

It is safe to say that from around 1890 or so until 1940 thereabouts he was doing business with the Saban sailors. Capt. Irvin Holm told Will Johnson in an interview that when he went to visit Mr. Kaliski he was lamenting the fact that he no longer saw his Saba friends whose interests he had been serving for many years. There were many old sailors' stories about Mr. Kaliski and his Saba headquarters at 27 South Street.

He got to know the Saba people and Saba so well that even though he had never been to the island he seemed to know every inch of it. He was a big joker as well. Captain Holm told Will that once he was in the store talking to Mr. Kaliski who had noticed Ainslee Peterson walking into the store. Kaliski had overheard both Ainslee and Wilson Johnson having heated arguments about sheep in the past. So he said to Capt. Holm: "It's a crying shame what Wilson has done."

That got Ainslee's attention right away! Kaliski went on to say that Wilson had gone down behind Old Booby Hill and shot all of the sheep that were there. Well, Ainslee was immediately ready to quit his job and to head down to Saba to deal with Wilson. Capt. Holm said it took a long time to convince Ainslee that Kaliski was only pulling his leg.

An interesting fact is that most of the descendants of Kaliski never moved to far away from their New York roots, and recently I was contacted by one of his great grand-daughters who was kind enough to provide a photo which after many years allowed us to put a face to that Angel whom looked over our Saba seamen for many years.

If you ever visit the Seaport Museum in New York, while there, say a prayer for the sweet repose of Mr. Hyman Kaliski a true friend of the Saban sailors of the past, Saba's former ambassador to the great City of New York and an angel to many of Saban descent.

OUR MEN OF THE 7 SEAS

The subject matter of this book has been treated from various perspectives by a number of distinguished authors in the various Caribbean territories. As such, it will be difficult to avoid treading over ground that will be familiar to some, particularly those more experienced and knowledgeable among us. This chapter will however attempt to review the parallels with updated information, which has been researched and, when possible, show the personal traits of our brave men at sea.

I don't know about you, but it seems to me that some generations back, people were in need to mature earlier. Nowadays you see big men hanging around street corners, running skateboards, or playing interactive games over internet, calling themselves 'the youth'. They could be somewhere doing useful work instead. Most of our Saban ancestors, by the age of 15 had been Cabin Boys for many of our Saban Captains in large schooners, and by nineteen some were already captains of inter-island trading schooners, able mariners or accomplished artisans and carpenters, building boats, and so on.

Amongst Saba's many celebrated records, the island has the particular merit of having produced over one-hundred licensed Captains of Schooners & Steamships, along with many 'coasters[1]' who nevertheless were sturdy men of sea and rightful captains of their own small vessels, whether sloops or row-boats. During WW I alone, it was estimated that around 135 captains from Saba were serving in the US Merchant Marine and on the Saban fleet of schooners, serving the rest of the Caribbean out of St. Kitts, Barbados, St. Thomas and other ports. In a census taken on Saba in the year 1912, out of a total male population of 774, no less than 530 (68%) were listed as seamen. The emigration of males and the establishment of permanent or semi-permanent homes abroad resulted in a population imbalance and Saba become known as an "Island of Women". As a matter of fact, in the 1940's "TRUE Magazine" sponsored a rather engaging short-film about the island, inciting viewers with

---

[1] Unlicensed captains of sloops, rowboats and other small crafts.

statements such as *"there are twenty unmarried women to each unmarried man"*, and suggested they were at their beckoning call if you were to visit the "Island of Women."

Overseas, Sabans became widely respected for their seafaring skills, earning them positions as captains and mates working for the major sea transportation companies of the era (such as Grace Line, Moore-McCormick, Red 'D' Line, etc.), as harbor masters and pilots at busy Caribbean ports at St. Thomas, Barbados, Bahamas, Santo Domingo as well as able seaman, engineers, oilers, firefighters and cooks.

Schooners were a very important part of inter-island trade of the Caribbean. Without these agile ships, which carried passengers and cargo, much of the Caribbean economy would have been hindered. Trading schooners had been coming to each Caribbean island for at least two-hundred years and engaged not only in the inter-island trade among the Caribbean islands, but also the trade with Canada and the eastern seaboard of the United States

In this chapter we include not only captains with masters' licenses who were captains of schooners and steamships, but also some notable "coasters" and seamen who assisted Saba, by providing services connecting people to visiting ships as well as to neighboring islands; the likes of politician *Matthew Levenston* who sailed mostly between Saba and St. Maarten, and *Captain Rudolph Dunkin* who maintained a steady trade between Saba and St. Kitts are just two examples of out brave coasters.

Although not all of them of them had an official title of Captain, they were certainly experts who learned to read the stars, use a sextant, a compass, feel the winds and navigate safely to their destinations. Once they put to sea, every man was the rightful captain of his own vessel.

Burials at Sea

As an inspiration by writers and artists, the sea is often romanticized. However, the experience of those who toiled to earn a living on the sea is far from romantic. Indeed, for centuries seamen have endured dangers and hardships. Out at sea, with seemingly endless workdays, their living conditions aboard the ship were riddled with difficulty.

In former times many of our sailors even found a grave at sea. The death registers are full of notices of men lost at sea or who died on their ships because of having caught yellow fever in Demerara, a storm at high seas, in one of the World Wars, and other places. Here is one of those notices:

"20 October 1886: Frederick Augustus Simmons (48) Captain of the Dutch schooner 'Rob' and Peter Hassell (49) boatsmen declared that at sea on October 10th at 5pm on board the "Rob" had died John William Johnson (34) born 1852, husband of Segesta Peterson, son of Richard Johnson and Elizabeth Leverock". (This notice also reflects the great variety of surnames on the island back in those days.)

In the death registers of Saba we can find an extract from the protocols of the Consulate of The Netherlands on Barbados which gives the account of the death of Peter Simmons, which was transcribed on August 14th 1910 (Folio #27):

"Extract from the protocol of the Consulate of The Netherlands in Barbados under date of July 1st 1909. On this first day of July 1909, there appeared before me Capt. Carty of the Sch. Trial, together with the following members of his crew: Edward Williams, Mate, William H. Howell, Cook, all of whom certified by their signatures attached breathen to the truth of the able Captain the statement, vis: Just at half past seven in the morning of the 28th day of June 1909, Captain Peter Simmons was going to take a sight when he was taken by with a fit of coughing which cause the blood to flow in every direction from mouth and nostrils. He got up and turned to the Mate, wiped the blood from his mouth and said 'look here'. He turned to go to the leeside which cause the Mate to fly from the wheel and go to his assistance. He died in the height of his bringing up the blood. He told Capt. Carty at 6 o'clock that same morning that the vessel was 220 miles to the North of the light ship, and 140 miles westward. From the time he began to bring up blood to when he dies was not five minutes. When the Mate had been holding up he mentioned his land to the Captain to turn back, which the Captain did without delay. He uttered nothing more. We kept liens on board until four o'clock and served him up in a tarpaulin with a bag full of stones to sink him away. We raised him and the cook read a few verses of the scriptures over him out of a sentiment and sadly and slowly we laid him unto his watery grave. We are all greatly shocked at the occurrence. The Sch Trial Sailed from Barbados on the 24th of June 1909 bound for Demerara and returned to Barbados the 30th of June 1909. In consequence of the death of navigator Peter Simmons. (Sgd) T. Carty, Captain; (sgd) Edward Williams, his + mark, Mate per V. C. Hanschell, (sgd) William H. Howell, Cook."

Will Johnson, in one of his articles, mentions the death of six Saban sailors: "After I wrote the original story I found out that Fernandus Jones was not buried in the same cemetery next to the house as Miss 'Cutchie' Jones. Actually he and Ronnie Johnsons' grandfather Frederick Zagers and three other men were on the 'Saba Bank' in a boat called the 'Why Not' in 1943 and they were lost at sea when a sudden storm came up and the small fishing boat was no match for the storm. Also Peter Woods, father of Ms. Edna Woods, was lost on that fatal night."

The event of a burial at sea was always a sad and solemn function. Unfortunately, one that for obvious reasons had to be in certain way rushed because the lack of refrigeration on certain type of ships. If the ship was expected at a port within a very short time, -within a day or two of the event-, they might wrap the body and wait until they docked so they could find a suitable resting place at a cemetery at the port of call. Many old sailor's, with plenty of salt in their veins, would have probably requested to have a burial at sea, in the land of the Mermaids!

My cousin Ashley Cordi publishes every year a press note with a personal version of the following poem, on behalf of her late grandmother "Nanny" Jordan (nee Simmons) to honor Capt. Harold Christopher Simmons and Capt. Cameron Dudley Simmons but it applies to all our seamen lost at sea:

There are no roses on sailors graves,
Nor wreaths upon the storm tossed waves,
No last post from the Royals band,
So far away from their native land,
No heartbroken words carved on stone,
Just shipmates bodies floating there alone,
The only tributes are the seagulls sweeps,
And the teardrop when a loved one weeps.

The body would be carried on deck to lie in one of the deck houses prior to burial which was often conducted quietly in the cold starry night, sometimes midnight, or in the early hours of the morning with the burial service being performed by a clergyman if there was one on board, or the master of the vessel. The four hours after midnight are called the "churchyard watch" or the second watch. As it was considered bad luck to carry coffins in an able schooner, the bodies were draped and sewn with a shroud of canvas or flag before they were consigned to the sea at the gangway. A precise record of the longitude and latitude would be recorded in the Captain's Log book. The mate might hold a lantern, while the doctor or his assistant held the bare coffin on the edge of the ship side. At a certain part of the service the body would be committed to the waves by the pronouncement of words in the tone of:

"May this sailor find repose in his final ship in which he gave his life that we may stay alive. Into thy hands, oh Lord, we commend the soul of your servant departed, now called on to eternal rest, and we commit his body to the deep."

Followed by the Lord's Prayer repeated and after ten minutes everyone would go back to their duties.

Capt. James Knight Simmons often told Will Johnson in a very emotional way how he had to bury his father at sea. Many Saban seamen lie in cemeteries throughout the West Indies and the world with unwritten epitaphs which would have revealed the drama and the glory of the life they led roaming the world.

In an Anglican church on the island of Bequia, in the Grenadines, a plaque on the wall reads: *"In memory of Captain Richard Hassell of Saba Island".* In a cemetery at Cayenne, French Guyana, are the graves of

Claude Mardenborough and Herbert Hassell of Saba who died of yellow fever while seeking their fortune in the goldfields.

Many more died at sea. The 'Maggie M. Hart', lost off Cape Hatteras on December 31st, 1902, had two Sabans on board: Edward C. Hassell and Alois Hassell, two of the many from Saba who were lost at sea.

On the other hand quite a few Sabans lost their lives on schooners torpedoed by the German U-boats in World War I. In one case alone George Rodney 'Mas Bowa' Johnson and Sarah Vlaughn lost four grandsons at one time on a schooner called the 'Bessie A. Crooks', which was lost on January 26th, 1917 in the Gulf of Pernambuco, Brazil: John Henry Johnson and his brother Lorenzo, James Hubert Every of Windwardside, and Norman Elmore Zeagers.

In World War II at least another twelve Sabans lost their lives on tankers torpedoed by the Germans. They were: Theophilus Wilson, lost December 31st, 1942 on Tanker 'Hermes'; John William Dunlock, torpedoed February 16th, 1942; also, Anthony Dudley Jackson; James Stewart Cornett; Walter A. Winfield; John Wilson; Darcy Kenneth Lynch; Reginald Gordon, died first half of March 1942 on British ship 'La Carriere'; James Edmund Gordon, December 1943; Carl Simmons, lost 1944 on 'Fern Castle'; Antonio Duran Woods, died on tanker 'Punta Gorda' on September 18th 1944; as well as Henry Swinton Woods.

Other old sailors were more fortunate and lived their final years in comfort of "The Sailors' Snug Harbor," an institution founded in 1801 by philanthropist Mr. Robert Richard Randall, a wealthy merchant and member of the Marine Society. In his will, he established a trust fund and donated a tract of land in Manhattan, which was made up of the Randall estate and an adjacent farm (Minto Farm), to become the first home of the Sailors' Snug Harbor. It was relocated to Sea Level, North Carolina in the early 1970's. Some of our sailors from Saba who lived their final days in that institution were: John Simmons, John Michael Dinzey Simmons, Hubert Lockland Heyliger, Herman Lawrence Every and Samuel Augustus Simmons Jr.

Coming to America

As we all know, many of our captains and men of sea migrated to the USA and other countries to provide a better life to their families, most of them on the back of their seafaring skills, but also as laborers, painters, carpenters, sail makers, cobblers and so on. They knew it would not be easy, but no one knew or expected additional problems to those they were leaving behind.

America, was a new land full of opportunities that would have its own set of challenges to test the mettle of our ancestors and their families. Granted, they had the benefit of not having to learn a new language which facilitated many things such as purchasing at stores and even getting a simple job. But socially, our ancestors had to deal with a more difficult subject such as inter-racial marriages although living in a society built upon immigrants.

Nevertheless, America was cruel, misunderstanding and judgmental. Especially Brooklyn, New York, in the 1940's and 1950's!! A tough atmosphere to bring their gentle brides and children not used to any kind of discrimination. Sometimes too white to be in a black community, sometimes too dark to be considered whites, they had to grow a very tough skin because they literally had to fight, almost daily, getting from home to school and back. There was strength in numbers so they started gathering, either by instinct or some unknown plan, in certain cities and places such as Richmond Hill, NY, Portland, MA and Providence, RI. Can you imagine the nun-nurses at a hospital, not wanting to hand-over a child, a little white infant, to his father, a big dark-skinned west-Indian man? Oh, the sundry struggles of many Saban families!

Marion's Balls

No book on Saba's captains and seamen would ever be complete without a mention to Marion Every, who orchestrated from her home above St. John's Village the movement of many people, including boatmen and porters, with her marine signals.

She 'manned' the signal station from high above on St. John's village. Mr. Alva Hassell, who grew up around Miss Marion, travelled once with Will Johnson to Curacao. As part of their conversation on many subjects, up came the topic of what the balls represented in this grapevine dialect. The explanation was as follows:

"When they were all horizontal it meant there was no vessel in sight. When in the distance a vessel was spotted, one ball was displayed vertically. This alerted the boatmen and porters in The Bottom to be ready if the boat was coming to Saba. As it got closer to the island a second ball was raised and a third one as it became clear that the vessel was indeed coming to Saba. When it went out of sight behind the hill the fourth one was raised so it was time to then rush down to

Fort Bay. If the vessel came in sight from behind 'Old Booby Hill' three balls were raised immediately, and then the fourth ball when the vessel went behind the hill above the Fort Bay. If it appeared that the vessel was not coming in to Saba then all four balls were immediately dropped into their permanent horizontal position."

All The Queen's Men

The coasters not only served as local anglers and the means of transportation of cargo, whether people or bulk packages, from the arriving ships to shore. They were also instrumental in proudly representing Saba on special occasions, such as the visits of dignitaries.

Saba-1957 - Visit Princess Beatrix - The boatmen waiting for the princess

Ernest Alfred Johnson

"No man can be sure of his courage until the day of his death".

"Men create real miracles when they use their God-given courage and intelligence." *Jean Marie Lucien Pierre Anouilh*

Ernest '21 Knots' Johnson

He was the second son of William James Johnson (1859-1905) and Judith Eleanor Dowling (1860-1905), born on Saba on June 15th 1884. He married Mary Ellen Hassell on December 19, 1906 and had four children: Lotty Grace, William Alfred, Mary Mildred and Gloria Madeline.

Famous for his rescue of the USS Submarine S-5 and for his unpublished manuscript[2] of his life and times at sea, he was very proud of his trajectory as a man of sea, where his real claim to glory was that he never lost a man or a ship to the ocean's embrace. Capt. Charles Reuben Simmons, who sailed with him as a mate for some time, said that Capt. Freddie was the best captain he ever sailed under.

---

[2] Life and Adventures of 21 Knots Johnson'

He immigrated to USA on June 12, 1901 via the port of New York and was naturalized at US District of Providence, RI on September 21st 1912. His good Saban friends, brothers Abraham & Carl Hassell, living at 56 Larch St., Providence, RI were his witnesses.

In his unpublished memoirs '*Life and Adventures of 21 Knots Johnson*', Captain 'Freddie' Johnson recounts with vivid intensity when he left Saba on the American schooner '*Priscilla*' under the command of Captain Thomas C. Vanterpool on January 20, 1902, headed for Humacao, Puerto Rico, to load cattle route to Guyana.

Four days later he arrived in Barbados to fetch water for the cattle, where he joined the schooner '*Daisy*' under the command of Matty Windfield of St. John's, and sailed the same day for St. Lucia to load a cargo of cord wood for Barbados. Later that year he joined Captain Lorenzo Simmons of The Bottom, and worked some months on the Windjammer '*Minerva*' transporting prisoners from Cayenne to Devil's Island and Maroni. It goes to show how Sabans got around. Capt. Johnson was also part owner of a large four-masted schooner.

No survivors

When a marine vessel goes down, unless it was a major catastrophe, there are often a few survivors between crew and passengers. However, when a submarine goes down, the report is usually "no survivors!" So it causes great surprise the events narrated by Capt. Ernest Alfred Johnson interviewed by Will Johnson, when in 1920, he participated in the rescue of a US Navy submarine some fifty-five miles off the coast of Delaware.

The USS S-5 was undertaking routine exercises with a new crew in preparation for the missions to come. During a crash-dive training, a ventilator was inadvertently left open and seawater flooded the forward torpedo room; the ship became nose-heavy, sank forward and dived to the ocean's floor. By the time they were able to shut it closed, they had the weight of over 80 Tons of water in the bow, hitting bottom with its nose buried in the silt of the ocean's bottom, and its stern angled upward. The water at this spot was 165 feet deep, but the submarine was 231 feet long, so its stern was sticking out of the water like a duck's tail searching for food. The pumps blew their gaskets trying to pump out water with a pressure of 150 pounds per square inch resisting them. Given the circumstances, chances for survival were certainly limited.

Captain Johnson was commanding the *USS Alanthus*, a 2,551 gross-ton wooden-hulled liberty freighter, which was built at Newark, NJ, in 1918 for the US Shipping Board's Emergency Fleet Corporation. However, as many of these ships at the end of WW I, she was not to see active naval service. Literally, the entire shipbuilding program of wooden freighters was destined to a short life.

In early September 1920, the USS *Alanthus*, was on its way to the scrap yard with a skeleton crew. While on her last voyage, she and her men were destined to perform an essential role during the rescue of the sailors trapped in the sunken submarine USS S-5.

A seaman on watch of the Alanthus spotted with his binoculars what he thought was a buoy. Knowing that no buoy should be so far out to sea, captain Ernest Alfred Johnson turned his vessel around to investigate.

The submarine had been disabled for over twenty-four hours before the Alanthus happened along. Inside the S-5, Captain Charles 'Saavy' Cooke and his crew had managed to drill a hole through the heavy steel hull plates and get some fresh air and push out a makeshift emergency flag they were waving.

Approaching the submarine's stern rising above the ocean, Capt. Johnson got in a small boat, advanced toward the sub and hailed the S-5 in maritime fashion. The conversation became legendary:

> *"Ahoy! What ship?"*
> **"S-5."**
> *"What nationality?"*
> **"American."**
> *"Where bound?"*
> **"Hell by compass!"**

The stern of the USS S-5 (left) protruding from the sea as the Alanthus stands by (Sept. 1920)[3]

He immediately had additional lines tied to the submarine to keep her from sinking, and rigged a deck pump in an attempt to pump fresh air and water to the crew trapped beneath the sea.

Due to the awkward angle that the ship was in, battery acid was leaking into the salt-water; fumes of gas began to climb up, taking up spaces of breathable air, beginning to suffocate the men in the sub. The *Alanthus* had a radio but no operator so they motioned a continuous S.O.S. signal with their flags and made pillowing smoke signals with oil, while crew members tried to enlarge the holes in the hull of the S-5. A Panamanian ocean liner, the *General Goethals*, arrived on the scene responding to the visual signals. Men from both ships, using power tools and pry bars, worked furiously to tear away the sub's hull plates. Around midnight they broke through.

[3] Photo NH57596 – Naval History & Heritage Command, Washington DC

Capt. Johnson had the foresight that when the men came out of the sub's hull, they would be exhausted from over 30 hours of lack of fresh air and the physical exertion of trying to get out, and would certainly need additional help to breach the gap between the ships and reach the safety of the Alanthus. While the final holes were being chipped away, he ordered several of his sailors to construct a "boatswain's chair.[4]" As the men came out of the S-5, they were secured and hoisted up, above the railing and gently deposited on the deck, using the ship's port-side derrick. As they arrived they were rushed to a small infirmary setup on the Alanthus and examined by the surgeons provided by the Goethals; most of them would receive hot coffee, soup, warm clothing and fresh blankets for each bunk that awaited them. Only four men suffered above average injuries: one with broken ribs and three with respiratory issues that merited additional care. Many of the men on the S-5 were traumatized, but all of them lived to see another day!

Freddie Johnson would later comment: "We are grateful we had such great weather during the time of the rescue, although we were in the peak of storm season." The rescue of the S-5 crew, even today, is the only known instance of a submarine sinking with a full crew and not one life being lost. (Bauman, 2000)

Subsequently, the Secretary of the Navy rewarded Captains Johnson and Swinson, and engineers Jakobsen, Grace, and McWilliams with golden watches engraved to commemorate the historic event and for their part in the rescue. Laid up after her arrival in port, the *Alanthus* disappeared from the Lloyd's shipping register after the 1922-1923 editions.

Hanging on display at the US Navy Yard in Washington, D.C., is a battered and scratched steel plate, two feet in diameter, edged with more than one hundred little semicircles. For more than ninety years, people have wondered how it came to be there and at the story it could tell. (Hill, 2010)

---

[4] A seat usually made of a board or canvas and a rope; used while working aloft or over the side of a ship.

Thomas James Darsey

Born on Saba the 29th of January of 1887, was the third son of Thomas Charles Darsey (1853-1921) and Aramintha Hassell (1854-1889). Before he came to the states he was living in Barbados with his soon to be brother in law Rupert Dowling, arriving on the SS Trinidad in April 1906. He became a naturalized citizen at the District Court of New York on Feb 6th 1917 and he enlisted as Second Mate in WW I. He was on a returning trip on the SS Catherine from St. Thomas, USVI with Ernest Hassell, oldest son of Henry Johnson Hassell and Lilly May Hassell (1872-1946).

On Jan 18th 1919 he is listed as the First Mate of the schooner George W Elzey Jr, arriving to the port of New York from Brazil. His address listed was 314 Green Ave, Brooklyn, NY which was the home of his sister Mary Ann Dowling.

As of the publication of this manuscript, I have not determined if he ever married nor his date and place of death.

William James 'Willy Witts' Hassell

He was the youngest son of Peter Carter Hassell (1808-1888) and Annie Johnson (1816-1889). He was born on June 15th 1845 and had two siblings: Ann Catherine and Henry Johnson Hassell. He married Eliza Jane Hassell (1848-1916), a daughter of James and Mary Ann Hassell, and they had seven children: Richard, John Benjamin, Oceana 'Doce', William James, David Waldron, Elsie and Eric Hassell.

He was the Captain of the barkentine sail ship "St. Peter" and the square rigger "R. L. T.", usually transporting coffee from Brazil to New York. In his early days, he would navigate with his family abroad, taking his wife and children.

He was a large husky man, but a gentile and considerate giant with his children. He would bring home food goods such as cake and beef, dresses for the girls, and sometimes pets like rare parrots and monkeys. When his son David became extremely sick he did everything he could to make his last moments as comfortable as possible. David was very fond of a horse he called 'Mora', a gift from his father, so the Captain took off the railing of the porch to the home so 'Mora' could stick her head through the window and say their goodbyes. That night, David passed away when only sixteen years of age.

"Willy Witts" suffered a debilitating stroke which affected his speech and hand skills, forcing him to retire. Bed-ridden to the end of his days, he was diligently attended to and supported by his loving wife Eliza Jane for all his needs. He died on February 2nd 1912.

Henry Johnson Hassell

Capt. Henry Johnson Hassell, aka "Henny Plunkie," was grandfather of, among others, the late Norman Hassell and his sister Marguerite Hassell. He was the owner of the large house which formed the main house of Captain's Quarters Hotel.

He was born on Saba about 1844, and married Johanna Beaks (1847-1883). Together they had seven children: Ann Mary, Amy, Mabel, Henry Johnson 'Mr. Heck', Ida, Peter James and John Lickens Hassell. Henry died about 1904.

James Knight Simmons

James Knight Simmons and his spouse aboard the SS Santa Barbara

He was born on October 26th, 1897 on Saba to Charles Simmons Jr. (1863-1910) and Peter Ann Every (1864-1946). His only sibling was the also well-known Captain Charles Reuben Simmons. He went to sea at age thirteen with his father Captain Charles Simmons who died on that same trip at sea with a high fever on the way back from Guyana to Barbados. Family lore states that the vessel becalmed just off Saba and it was decided to bury him at sea. A breeze sprang up immediately after and within half an hour the vessel was in port at Saba.

Captain James Knight Simmons attended the Navigation School on Saba and then moved on to the United States where he learned steamships. He was captain for the Grace Line Company for many years and navigated mostly between New York and South America. During World War II, he took part in D-Day and his ship was scuttled at Omaha Beach in France.

Captain Knight used to call in to Aruba and Curacao with the "SS Santa Rosa". He sailed as captain with the company for over thirty years. The old "Santa Rosa" carried about 50 passengers in storage and 209 in first class. She started sailing on November 26th 1932. Late 1936 Grace Lines acquired the Red 'D' Line, which also had a number of Saba captains in its day. The service was between New York, Venezuela, Curacao, Colombia,

Cristobal Panama and Haiti. The 'Santa Clara', renamed the 'Susan B. Anthony', was sunk in the Normandy when she struck a mine that exploded under her #4 hold, leaving her powerless and with a stuck rudder. I don't know if he was captain of her at the time.

Among the Grace Line ships, he was captain of were the "Santa Rosa", the "Santa Barbara" and the "Santa Clara." His last command was the "SS. Margarita".

Captain Knight was married to a German lady named Helen. They had a daughter and a son, Ruth Ann and James Charles, who live in the United States. He lived to be 95 and died in 1992.

James Stewart Cornett

He was born on Saba, 29 August 1904, the third son of John Busby Cornet and Antonietta Simmons. He married Dora Madeline Jones from St. Johns, Saba on July 19th 1926 and has one daughter Emily Lucy Agatha Cornet.

He was an Able-Bodied Sailor, on oil tanker Pedernales, Lago Shipping Co. (UK)

He died in the Caribbean Sea on February 16th 1942 when the tanker he was working on was torpedoed and sunk by German U-boat U-156, at anchor near San Nicolas, Aruba.

James Carlton 'Opa' Riley

He was the youngest child born on November 10th 1928 to James Allen Riley (1886-1966) and his wife Elsie Lottie Riley (1888-1977), who were married on Saba on June 23rd 1920. His siblings were: Thelma Mildred, Frank Oliver, Gladys Florine, Maud Viola and Willam Oscar Riley.

He grew up in the area known as Promised Land. As many children of the day, education started at home "the right way". Solid principles went a long way. From humble homes children were taught to be polite, treat people with respect, be honest, friendly and tidy would take you a long was, especially with strangers; you never knew where you would go in the future! His lifetime hard work and experience provided him with a simple life philosophy which he transmitted to his children: *"Daddy never come up easy, so Daddy ain't going to bring you up easy!"*

At seven years old he was already helping his father handling the donkeys, driving them up and down to the beach with cargo arrived. After school he would also cut grass to feed them and make sure they had water.

As many youngsters from Saba, he had the dream to follow his brother to sea, becoming an engineer on a steam ship and be out at sea for months at a time.

At seventeen he went to sea on sloops and schooners from Saba to St. Maarten, St. Kitts, St. Barths and Statia with Captain Dunkin and Capt. Levenston. He sailed for about a year and then he started working at the Bay as a porter and also as a cargo checker. He also worked with Nederville Heyliger on the harbor master ship. In 1963 the Executive Council appointed him as harbor master under the condition that he would "dress up." After measuring the pros and cons, he accepted the assignment.

As he confessed to Julia G. Crane while she was writing her book "Saba Silhouettes", October 14th 1955 marked his life forever and for the better as he embraced his Christian faith and served the Lord.

A lady from Nevis arrived with her cousin, who was related to a local pastor on Saba. While attending church 'Opa' introduced himself to Albertine Taylor and it was love at first sight, at least for him. After a few visits to church, he told her he loved her. It came time to leave to home on the ship *Gloria* going to St. Kitts. As luck would have it, Riley was working on it as well. While at sea, he made sure he spoke more and more with her. He knew she had nowhere to go so she had to listen. Finally he got to write a letter to her parents and within a year they were engaged. He married Albertine Taylor from Nevis, British West Indies on Saba on December 23rd 1958 and they had four children.

Carlton Riley died on November 3rd 2010.

John William Dunlock

John W. Dunlock was born on Saba of February 3rd, 1905. He married Mary Cassaline Hassell (1903-2005) and had three children: Elfreda Louise, Holma Winifred and Marianne Hortence Dunlock.

He worked as Quartermaster on the oil tanker Tia Juana working for Lago Shipping Co. (UK)

Died on February 16, 1942 when the ship SS Oranjestad was torpedoed and sunk by German submarine U-502 in the Gulf of Venezuela.

Solomon 'Butchie Coonks' Simmons

Capt. Solomon Simmons

Capt. Solomon Simmons was a first cousin of James Horton Simmons. Their fathers, John and Charles respectively, as well as Phoenix, Abraham, Peter George and others were all brothers. Charles married Alice Eliza Horton from Hell's Gate village whose father, James Horton, was the owner of good farm land on Hell's Gate and he moved over there. It still has not been determined with factual data about the use of the name "Coonks" as a nickname in both male and female members of this branch of the Simmons family. We have also seen Mary Simmons referred to in the property registers as Mary "Coonks" Simmons. Sylvester Hughes used to say that as a boy he lived by 'Redhead Joe' Simmons, and that the old timers would tease the children telling them that "Coonks and Cuvelje are coming to get you" in reference to the famed pirate captains. I guess they were not the nicest of fellers if you used their names to frighten little children with.

According to his daughter's (Edna Blanche) passport application, Solomon immigrated to USA about 1895 and lived in USA for 17 years (uninterruptedly) in Brooklyn NY; he was naturalized citizen at Eastern District Court of Brooklyn on Dec 2, 1911.

He was born on Saba in 1851 and married Ann Rebecca Horton (1849-1932) on June 13th 1874. They had five children: Solomon Conrad, Eliza Jane, Eloise, John and Joseph Hilton. Only on his deathbed did Captain Simmons confess to his Saba family that he had a second family in Montego Bay, Jamaica.

Eugenie Bruce and Solomon Simmons, had four daughters and one boy: Carmen Sylvia, Sydney Augustus, Enid May, Edna Blanche and Ernestine who was called 'Teena'. Enid May eventually became the wife of Commodore Thomas Simmons and Edna Blanche married Capt. Cameron Dudley Simmons.

According to my late cousin Edna Louise Brown (nee Simmons), Solomon died in Kingston, Jamaica in 1912 and Eugenie died in 1917. His son, Captain Johnny Simmons together with his sister Eliza Jane Simmons went in search of the Jamaican branch of the family and took the three youngest girls to New York, two of which eventually married Sabans. The son remained in Jamaica with his older sister, and lived to be a very old man. Carmen remained in Jamaica due to a pregnancy; she eventually followed and went to Lenox Hill Hospital Nursing School in New York.

Reginald Gordon

He was the oldest son of James Edmond Gordon and Ophelia Jackson. He was born on November 28th 1914 in Hell's Gate, Saba.

Although officially he did not work as a seaman, he was aboard many ships as Second Cook, SS La Carriere, Trinidad Leaseholds Ltd.

He died on 25 February 1942 when ship was torpedoed and sunk by German submarine U-boat (U-156), south-west of Puerto Rico.

Charles Reuben Simmons

Capt. Charles Reuben Simmons

Charles Reuben Simmons, born on September 27, 1895 on Saba to Charles Simmons Jr. (1863-1910) and Peter Ann Every (1864-1946), left his beloved island as a young man for the United States. There he attended navigation school at White Hall Street in New York City. He obtained his license as second Mate, later he became First Mate, and then he obtained his Masters license.

While he was a Quartermaster on board the 'Missouri' he was torpedoed off Genoa, Italy in the Mediterranean on April 4th 1917, and spent several days at sea before being rescued. This ship was under the command of Captain Hilton Simmons of The Bottom and belonged to the American Hawaiian Lines. Menthor Hassell of Windwardside was First-Mate, Earl Simmons of The Bottom was Quarter-Master and Peter 'Petie' Johnson was also a sailor. Other ships on which he sailed were the 'Sea Breeze' and the 'Steadfast'.

The first ship under his full command was the schooner "Mayflower"; she was 147 feet long and weighed 190 tons. Built for speed in Gloucester, Massachusetts it was fabricated to compete in the "Bluenose" races. He sailed as her Captain, from 1928 to 1930. In conversations with Will Johnson, he confessed that in 1929 he left St. Kitts with 375 passengers and 48 hours later landed them at Curacao. He once carried 460 passengers from Dominica and St. Lucia with this schooner and was promptly fined upon arrival at his port of call for carrying too many passengers! Considering he made a huge profit from the overload of passengers, the fine was promptly paid. On return trips to the Windward Islands he carried as many as 100 people. The least amount of passengers he ever carried to Curacao was 110 from Dominica. Every fifteen days he would make the run to carry workers for the oil refinery there.

The "Three Sisters" was a three-masted schooner which had been purchased by Capt. William Benjamin Hassell, in 1927, and was 190.76 tons and 115 feet long, took over the mail service in 1929 and was the last of the Saba owned mail schooners to ply the trade between the Dutch islands.

Other ships on which he sailed were the 'Sea Breeze' and the 'Steadfast.' He was also First Mate on the five-masted 'T.N. Barnsdell', under the command of legendary Ernest Alfred Johnson. Between 1940 and 1944 he was a pilot in Demerara.

The "Antilia" was the last ship that Captain Charles Reuben Simmons sailed on.

After his sea faring days he lived on Saba. He used to own the former Utilities building in The Bottom. He sold it to Chief Police constable the late Bernard Halley, and when he died the family sold it to a Mr. Claude Wathey.

On Tuesday August 30th, 1993 Captain Charles Reuben Simmons, who was born on September 27th 1895 passed away at the Home For The Aged. He was the last of the old breed of sea captains who made Saba proud in days gone by. His father was a Captain as well as his brother Capt. James Knight Simmons who recently passed away in New York. Their father Charles died at sea after picking up yellow fever on a trip to Demarara to bring cargo to Barbados. He was buried at sea. His son Knight, only 13 at the time, had to make the decision to bury his father at sea. The moment the body hit the water a wind came up and in less than no time they were at Saba. Capt. Reuben left Saba as a young boy, fatherless.

He went to a school of navigation at White Hall Street in New York City. There he obtained his license as a second mate, later he became first mate, and then he obtained his Masters license. The first ship under his command was the schooner the 'Mayflower', owned by Capt. Tommy Vanterpool. While quarter-master on board of the 'Missouri' he was torpedoed off Genoa in the Mediterranean on April 4th, 1917, and spent several days at sea before being rescued. This ship was under the command of his cousin, Captain Hilton Simmons of The Bottom, and belonged to the American Hawaiian Lines. Menthor Hassell of Windwardside was first mate, Earl Simmons of The Bottom was Quarter Master and Petie Johnson was also a sailor. Other ships on which he sailed were the 'Sea Breeze' and the 'Steadfast'. He was also first mate on the four masted "T.N. Barnsdell" under the command of Capt. Ernest Alfred Johnson of Booby Hill. Between 1940 and 1944 he was a pilot in Demarara.

He leaves to mourn his daughter Miss Estelle Simmons of Zions Hill, also a number of nephews and nieces among whom Freddie, Eric, Guy and Will Johnson. God blessed him with a long life and he was privileged in the line of his work to know many lands and many people and he always considered himself blessed by his experiences all over the world.

John Roy Peterson

Roy Peterson became captain of steamships and tankers. He was a son of Daniel Peterson (1819-1888) and Elenor Peterson (1825-1907), born on December 25th, 1903 at Windwardside, Saba. His siblings were brother of Alma, Vivian, Lovell Clyde, James Clifton, Ethelbert, Phillip and Grace Peterson.

His name appears on the roll List for the Saba Navigation School in January 1920. When he first went to New York he worked with Captain George Irvin Holm on the SS 'Edith' and SS 'Clare' of the Bull Insular Line, which plied the waters between New York and Caribbean ports such as Curacao, Aruba, Puerto Rico, St. Kitts among others. Many other Sabans worked on that same ship. He also worked in several capacities on the SS Agwisun of the Ward Line. He served aboard the SS Dillwyn of J. D. Mallory Lines as Second Mate. He became master of the liberty oil tanker "Christopher L Sholes" for the Southeastern Oil Delaware Company working for Lago Oil Aruba.

He was naturalized by the Supreme Court, State of New York in Long Island on December 21, 1927. He suffered a heart attack and died in a New York subway while only in his forties. He died on April 19th, 1935.

Stanley Isadore Johnson

Stanley Isadore Johnson

Stanley Johnson was born on February 6, 1890 to Rebecca Elizabeth Vlaun (1862-1939) and John George Johnson (1862-1942) on Saba. As many Sabans before him, he first set sail on various local schooners at the age of fourteen, traveling through the various West Indian Islands. He sailed with local captains including Knight Simmons, Benjamin Hassell, Thomas Vanterpool and Augustine Johnson.

In 1910 he was already sailing through the West Indies on the schooner "The Dreadnought" with Capt. Knight Simmons and Captain Tommy Vanterpool. Because Capt. Tommy was a wanted man in Cayenne for smuggling escaped prisoners from Devil's Island, when the schooner went there Captain Tommy remained in Barbados or elsewhere. In 1912 Stanley went to New York and sailed out on large schooners throughout the world. When Will Johnson interviewed him he was 95 years old and could not remember the names of those first schooners he sailed on.

He sailed with his first cousin Edward Johnson who died in 1984 at the age of 96 in New York. Edward was married to Lucille Hassell who was the aunt of Capt. Eddie Hassell of the Swinging Doors restaurant in Windwardside. On January 2nd, 1922 he married Alice Eliza Simmons (1902-1999) daughter of James Horton Simmons and Agnes Johnson.

At the age of thirty-seven, Stanley sailed to the United States aboard the SS Caracas arriving at Ellis Island in New York on April 13th, 1927. Along with him on the steamship were six other men from Saba: Reuben Johnson (age 45), David O. Johnson (age 16), William Johnson (age 36), Moses Johnson (age 52), David Johnson (age 17) and Richard Johnson (age 45). The official Ellis Island Ship's Manifest indicates that all seven men listed their destination as 27 South Street, in lower Manhattan. This was the address of the Sabans' godfather for over fifty years, Mr. Hyman Kaliski, a German-Jewish merchant. He and his wife operated a boarding house and clothing store which was primarily used by sailors from Saba during their stays in New York.

After arriving in New York in 1927, Stanley was not to return to Saba until 1936. During those nine years he sailed for four years on the four-masted schooner "Albert F. Paul", with Captain Southard and his wife Ruby, who were like family to him. The Albert F. Paul sailed from Nova Scotia and the New England fishing grounds to the Gold Coast of Africa. It was later sunk by a U-Boat (U-332) on March 13, 1942 about 160 miles north-northeast of Cape Hatteras.

The other schooners upon which Stanley sailed carried various goods and products as diverse as corned codfish from New Bedford, Massachusetts and potatoes from Long Island, to salted cowhides from Brazil. He traveled around the Cape of Good Hope in South Africa and the Horn of

Africa while sailing for Moore-McCormack Lines and Kerr McGee. During these years he also sailed the inland waterways, particularly the Hudson, from the St. Lawrence Seaway to New York harbor. He sailed on the Georgia, the Tennessee, and the Mohawk, carrying timber down the Hudson.

After sailing inland for several years he returned to the sea, sailing out of Mobile, Alabama, and New Orleans, Louisiana for the Waterman Steamship Company of Boston, Massachusetts. During this nine year period sailing out of New York, he, as many other Saba men, decided to become an American citizen. On March 17, 1932, while still listing his residence as 27 South Street in New York he was sworn in as a United States citizen. His decision was based in large part because of the opportunities the United States had provided to him.

In 1936, he returned to Saba and sailed again on local schooners. He remained on Saba until shortly after the death of his beloved mother Rebecca, in 1939. He never had the opportunity to see his homeland again. Not long after his return to the United States, World War II began.

He sailed with the Seafarer's International Union as a Merchant Marine. As such, he sailed on unarmed cargo ships in convoys to Europe and Russia, bringing aid and much needed supplies. Will Johnson had the opportunity to stay at his home in Richmond Hill for two months in the winter of 1967. Will recalls him telling stories about how cold it was in Murmansk, Russia. If you made the mistake and held on to the rail, your hand would stick to it.

During the war he frequently sailed on the SS "Robin Tuxford" under Captain Kenneth Chamberlain. Along with him on the ship was Stanley's first cousin, Edward Johnson, who served as Chief Engineer. This ship made numerous trips following the "Murmansk Run", an Artic Sea route where merchant ships steamed into the most northerly open waters of the stormy Artic to reach ports in Russia, avoiding the feared U-Boats and battling bone piercing chills and eternal gray skies. This supply route was absolutely vital to the Russians in their hold against the Nazi offensive.

Stanley also sailed on the SS "Graylock," which was sunk off the coast of Murmansk in 1943. He and his shipmates were rescued by a British

Corvette and brought to Glasgow, Scotland, where they remained for some months recovering from pneumonia. Stanley also had the unfortunate luck of having another ship torpedoed by a German U-boat off the New England Coast.

As a result of his service to the United States, Stanley was awarded four service medals, including two for service in the Atlantic War zone. The United States did not, however, issue these medals until decades after his service, because Merchant Marines were not traditionally recognized for their war time service, since they were considered civilian. This oversight was corrected by the U.S. Government in the 1980's and these brave men received the honors they deserved.

Stanley Johnson also received a medal of honor from the Russian government for his service in the convoys which brought life-saving supplies to the ports of Murmansk and Arch Angel during the war. He was honorably discharged from the US Maritime Service on August 15, 1945. During his fifty plus years at sea, Stanley sailed to the ports of Africa, Asia, Europe, South America and North America and was devoted to the sea. Upon his final retirement from the sea, he lived out his remaining years in Richmond Hill, New York with his wife Alice, his children Bessie, Carl Lester and Arlene and his beloved grandchildren.

He died peacefully at the age of 98 on April 7, 1988.

John Simmons

Capt. John 'Johnny' Simmons was a son of Solomon 'Butchie Coonks' Simmons (1851-1912) and Ann Rebecca Horton (1849-1932) born at The Botton, on Saba on March 21st 1879. His siblings were Solomon Conrad, Eliza Jane, Elouise and Joseph Hilton Simmons who was also a captain. He was half-brother of Carmen Sylvia, Sydney Augustus, Enid May, Edna Blanche and Ernestina Simmons all from Jamaica.

He first put out to sea in 1895 aboard the British schooner "Racer" from Demerara to Martinique. In October 1897 he was a sailor aboard the American Schooner "James Slater" from Demerara to Philadelphia; he spent the next 24 years at sea in several positions working on ships for the America Hawaiian Line.

He married to Fredericka Haddock from St. Thomas about early 1900's and was the father of two daughters and one son: Elsie E., Robert Eric and Amy A. Simmons.

He was naturalized as US Citizen on January 9th 1901 by the US District Court of Brooklyn, NY. Between 1917-1919 he served as in the US Navy as Lt. Commander assigned to the Third Naval District while he had his residence at Great Kills, NY.

His career of 26 years of serving on sea-going vessels included 23 years on Merchant Off-shore vessels, aboard schooners and steamships, including his tenure with the Navy. The last part of his maritime career was aboard steamships providing coastal services in the USA. In 1935 he was Second-Mate aboard the merchant vessel SS Verinar.

In August 1935 he was suffering from several ailments and was declared "physically unfit to serve", at which time he applied and was accepted at the Sailor's Snug Harbor. He recovered and was able to go back to sea and his last assignment was as a Fire Watchman aboard the SS "American Importer" and the "President Harding", plying in the European trade.

In 1937, he was again interned at the Sailor's Snug Harbor with heart complications. He died at their hospital on December 24th 1941.

Joseph Hilton Simmons

A son of Solomon 'Butchie Coonks' Simmons (1851-1912) and Ann Rebecca Horton (1849-1932) born at The Botton, on Saba on November 25th 1882.

His first official job at sea was aboard the American schooner "D. J. Sawyer" as an Able Seaman and worked for companies such as the New York and Cuba Mail Steamship Co's, and the Dixie Steamship Co. out of Galveston, Texas. Between 1909 and 1913 he worked on several steamers of the Cuba Mail Steamship Co., having served as First, Second and Third

Officer and in his recommendations he is referred to as "a competent and efficient officer and a man of correct habits." Other companies he worked for were the Continental Trading Co., US Steamship Co., Federal Line, Oriental Navigation Co., US Shipping Board where he worked in the capacity of Port Captain, Frances & Canada Steamship Corp., Merchant & Miners SS Company, and the Texas Mediterranean Line.

Some of the ships he commanded were the steamship 'Owego' among others. Also on the SS Olympic, arriving Jul 28, 1920; His listed address on this trip is 811 St. John's Place, Brooklyn, NY.

Traveling on the SS Esperanza on Oct 11, 1913 he clearly stated his birth date as Nov 24, 1882; he listed his address as 8 Fulton St, NYC

After the death of his father Capt. Solomon Simmons, Hilton was appointed the ward of his three young half-sisters Enid May, Edna Blanche 'Nan' and Ernestina 'Teena' Simmons and was involved in bringing them to USA, daughters of his father with Eugenia Bruce from Montego Bay, Jamaica who had also died.

In the early 1920's he began to suffer diabetic ailments and deafness which complicated his seafaring life.

He was the Master aboard the SS "West Ekonk" on January 14th 1931 on a round trip from Galveston, Texas to Genoa, Italy. At the age of 50, he was living at the Scottish Rite Temple in Galveston, TX when he requested asylum at the Sailor's Snug Harbor in 1933. However, he resigned and was released without prejudice in November 1943 to be an active participant in World War II.

His last command was in July 1947 as Third Office of the American steamship "Townsand Harris" from Philadelphia, PA to ports in South America, South Africa, Europe and back to the port of New York.

In May 1950 he was again accepted again at the facilities of Sailor's Snug Harbor. He accumulated a total of 34 years at sea. He died in April 1966 in DuPage, IL.

Herman Lawrence Every

Although a full-fledged sailor who could lend a hand in the most critical moments, Herman Every was the man responsible to make sure that that captains and the crew were well fed. His entire 36 years at sea, he worked as a Cook and Steward aboard the large wooden vessels.

He was born on Saba on March 16th 1869; her parents were John and Mary Every and he had one sister, Rose Ellen Every. As many Saban boys he started out as a cabin boy but took pride in developing his culinary skill at the service of many captains such as Ernest Alfred 'Freddie' Johnson and Arthur Wallace Simmons. He worked aboard the schooner "Charles G. Endicott" as Cook and Steward; he was also employed on the schooners "Helen L. Martin", "D. H. Rivers", "Margaret Throop" and the "Edward H. Blake". His first large commission was on May 1898 aboard the Schooner "N. H. Skinner" on a coastwise voyage sailing out of New York. By the end of his career, he was traveling aboard the SS Mayan to the West Indies and Central America from the Port of New Orleans and worked six months at the Oak Island Fishing Camp.

All his fellow captains would sincerely praise him in recommendation letters as "a man of fine character, with no bad habits and deserving," "during his time with me as a cook and steward, his services were entirely satisfactory and I take pleasure in recommending him as such." His certificate of service was signed by Saba's best friend, Hyman Kaliski.

His sunset was at the Sailor's Snug Harbor institution on February 25th 1943 at 5:30pm. The institution notified his friends Captains Ralph and George Holm.

John Michael Dinzey Simmons

He was the youngest son of Capt. Isaac Simmons (1840-1886) and Ann Dinzey (1842-1911), born at The Bottom, Saba on January 1st 1880. Aparently he married a woman from Barbados, Teddy Axelson, however by the time we finalized this edition of the book, we had not found specific information about her; nevertheless, we do know from documents at the Sailors' Snug Harbor that at the time of his admission to the institution, he had an eight year old son named Oswald D. Simmons.

As most Sabans, he started off working on large sailboats such as the schooner "D. H. Rivers" (Arthur W. Simmons, Master), the schooner "E. Starr Jones" (H. L. Hassell) and the schooner "Gracebell Tyler" (S. A. Simmons Sr). He also was the captain of the Schooner "James Slater" and "Racer". He had a total of 19 years of experience, having been the First-Mate of several large steamers such as SS Zulia, the French American Line's SS Shooters Island, and the SS Western Pride of the Luckenbach Steam Co.

The sea was not kind to him or his body. By the age of 52 he had been certified by his doctors to be physically disabled. He was accepted into the Sailors' Snug Harbor on July 22nd 1932 and he died on March 8th 1936 of cardiac failure.

Charles Ferius Hassell

Charles was born on Saba, July 1st 1863 a son to Johanna Hassell (the same day as the emancipation of the slaves on Saba). He was a freedom child who later lost his life in an event which caused the Spanish-American war.

The report of his death contains the following information, which should be of interest to our readers:

Name of deceased: Charles Ferius Hassell. Rank: Gunners Mate, 3rd class. Date of death February 15th, 1898. Place of death: Havana. Cause of death: Asphyxia ex submersion. The document further states: "I hereby certify that Charles F. Hasell, Gunners Mate 3rd class, U.S. Navy, died while attached to the U.S.S. "Maine". Death occurred in the harbor of Havana, Cuba on the night of February 15th, 1898, as the result of an explosion and the sinking of the U.S.S. "Maine". Record of deceased: Native of Saba, West Indies, Age 34 years, 7 months, Height 5 feet 10 inches. Complexion: Negro. Where enlisted: New York. When enlisted; April 25th, 1895. Previous service: about 5 years and 2 months. First enlisted: January 21ˢᵗ, 1889.

His mother Johanna was 70 at the time of his death. That same year an application was made on her behalf by the local Kings Council and Notary, Engle Heyliger Simmons for a pension. Also the Government schoolmaster Mr. R. L. Hassell, wrote a letter on her behalf to the Commissioner of Pensions. A general affidavit had the following information: Moses Johnson and Lovelock Hassell had appeared before the Notary and declared the following: "that they had been personally acquainted with the person Charles F. Hassell, native of this island, son of Johanna Hassell, late Gunners Mate on the U.S. ship "Maine", from his earliest youth, that he never married on this island, and that to the best of their knowledge and belief was never married in any other place, and that at his death he left no widow nor minor child."

His mother, Mrs. Johanna Hassell, was taken care of by Henry Johnson Hassell ("Henny Plunkie"), a Captain and owner of the house which used to be the cornerstone building of the "Captain's Quarters" Hotel. She died on April 30th, 1913 and was around 88 years of age.

Lawrence Almonde Hassell

He was the second son of Richard Lovelace Hassell (1864-1900) and Ann Catherine Hassell (1867-1913), born on Saba April 6ᵗʰ 1890. His siblings were Richard Carl Athelstan, Elaine, Mabel and Edwin Hassell. He married about 1921 to Margarette L. McKeefe from New York and had one child: Lawrence Hassell. They lived at 761 Prospect Pl, Brooklyn, NY.

He was naturalized on Nov 18th 1914 at the Southern District Court of New York. He provided his services during WW I where he had the rank of Lieutenant of US Navy and saw action with cargo and transport ships to London.

He worked for many years first at the American Hawaiian Steamship Co., and then became an Officer for W. R. Grace & Co. staring as Third Mate on the SS Mineola where he moved on to Second Mate in 1923. He was also Master of the following ships: SS Henry George (1943), SS Floridian (1945), SS Dickinson Victory (1946), and SS Jacob A. Westervelt (1949) sailing to ports as far as Kobe, Japan and Milne Bay, Papua New Guinea.

He died on Jan 21st 1978 in Albany, NY.

Edwin Hassell

He was the youngest son of Richard Lovelace Hassell (1864-1900) and Ann Catherine Hassell (1867-1913). His siblings were Richard Carl Athelstan, Lawrence Almonde, Elaine, and Mabel. He married about 1927 to Helen (?) from New York and had five children: Edwin, Bernadette, Richard, Bernard and Lawrence.

He participated in World War I as a sailor; he worked as a sailor on the SS Atenas (1915), and eventually became Third Mate on the SS Sagaporack (1922), Chief Officer of the SS Golden Tide (1931) and SS Panaman of the American Hawaiian Lines.

The American-Hawaiian Steamship Company was founded in 1899 to carry cargo of sugar from Hawaii to the United States, and manufactured goods back to Hawaii. Brothers-in-law George Dearborn and Lewis Henry Lapham were the key players in the founding of the company.

At the time of the company's founding, its steamships sailed around South America via the Straits of Magellan to reach the East Coast ports. By 1907, the company began using the Isthmus of Tehuantepec Route. Shipments on the Tehuantepec Route would arrive at Mexican ports— Salina Cruz, Oaxaca, for eastbound cargo, and Coatzacoalcos, Veracruz for westbound cargo—and would traverse the Isthmus of Tehuantepec on the Tehuantepec National Railway. When American political troubles with Mexico closed that route, American-Hawaiian returned to the Straits of Magellan route.

When the Panama Canal opened for traffic in August 1914, American-Hawaiian began routing all of its ships via this route. The temporary closure of the canal because of a series of landslides forced the company to return to the Straits of Magellan route for the third time in its history.

During World War I, twelve of the company's ships were commissioned into the United States Navy; a further five were sunk by submarines or mines during the conflict.

Roger Dearborn Lapham, a future mayor of San Francisco, California, served as company president in the mid-1920s.

During World War II, the company operated many Liberty ships and Victory ships under the War Shipping Administration, including the Daniel Boone, the John Milledge, the John Drake Sloat, the Benjamin Goodhue and the Chanute Victory.

Edwin died on June 3rd 1982.

Richard Hassell

In researching for information, one finds some eloquent descriptions of facts as lived by their actors that it would be a pity to try to put it in other words. The following was written by Richard Stewart Hassell when he was 87 years of age and living in Santa Monica, CA.; he was a grandson of Capt. Richard Hassell, and the stories are described as they was relayed to him by his mother Lily May Hassell whom in turn received the stories from her mother Ann Rebecca Hassell. With the intention to preserve verbal meme as it is transmitted from one generation to the next, here is what he wrote:

"My grandfather, Captain Richard Hassell, was born on the tiny Dutch island of Saba (only 5 miles square in size) in the year 1856. His forbearers settled on Saba in the year 1640.

Since seafaring was the way of life in those days, and the island being so small, the male population by necessity had to go to sea in order to earn a living and support their families. The very young teenagers had to start out going to sea at 13 years of age to follow in their father's footsteps, and were always signed on the ship as the "cabin boy." It was standard practice that the captain had the responsibility of teaching the cabin boy all the rest of the schooling he would be missing by starting out at sea at such an early age. In addition he had to teach him all the rudiments of navigation and seamanship, along with the aid of books on the subject.

As it turned out, my grandfather was a very ambitious man, and so at 16 years of age he decided that he wanted to get married and so he married a Saban girl, who happened also to be 16, after receiving the blessings of her parents. One year later my mother was born. Being a father gave my grandfather the impetus to learn more about navigation and seamanship. He studied so hard that at age 21 he had taken the examination for a Captain's license and passed it, whereupon the shipping company for which he was sailing gave him command of a ship, and so he kept going to sea. It was a customary thing for a shipping company not to allow the prospective captain to take command of a ship without being a part owner, which was 25% of what the ship was worth. The shipping company's idea was that the captain of the vessel would be more interested in keeping it in good shape and would look out more for the company's interest, if he was a part owner. My grandfather turned out to be a man of good judgment and thrifty with his money, because he had built his own home on the island of Saba by the time my mother was three years old. After having sailed to New York many times, my grandfather decided to take his family to live there in the year 1877. After their first son Richard was born, my grandmother started to get a little more apprehensive about my grandfather going to sea, particularly after having weathered three hurricanes at sea. He finally relented and found a grocery store in New York City that was for sale and bought it almost immediately. But being a born seaman at heart, he put the grocery store up for sale after only two years and eventually sold it to another merchant. He found a small schooner of 46 tons in size and bought it, putting it in seaworthy shape. He began trading up and down the East Coast of the United States and the Caribbean area. He called the vessel the R. H.

My mother, having been born in 1872, was about 8 years of age and interested in whatever my grandfather did, because my grandmother had gotten in the habit of keeping her informed even at such a young age, particularly about the dangers of going to sea. Although Captain Hassell had some dangerous adventures, one where he was the only survivor, he always returned successfully. But my grandmother was more convinced than ever that she should try to persuade him to give it up. Finally, in about 1886, on a particular trip to Jacksonville, Florida, he was approached by a representative of a local shipping company who was interested in buying the R. H. at a price satisfactory to my grandfather. By the following day he found out that an orange grove was for sale located on the St. John's River, not too far from Jacksonville. The price of the orange grove was much less than what he had been offered for the R. H. and so he made up his mind to sell his beloved ship and buy the orange grove.

So he put down a down payment on the orange grove and signed an agreement to sell the R. H. to the shipping company, advising them that he would have to go back to New York City and conclude all business there before returning to Jacksonville and finalizing the sale of the R. H. and purchasing the orange grove. Captain Hassell finally got all the business taken care of in New York and took enough supplies, including food and water for 26 days to take him and his family to Jacksonville. After about 3 days at sea, when he was approximately off the coast of Cape Hatteras, the vessel's barometer started to fall rapidly. From his experience with other hurricanes he knew that the telltale signs pointed to trouble – running headlong into another hurricane. He immediately called the crew together and told them that from his past experience with hurricanes he felt it imperative that they prepare. He decided to ride it out. He then ordered the crew to take in all sails except for the jib which he needed to help keep the vessel's bow into the wind. He battened down the hatches. He further asked several crew members to lash him to the helm, so that he would not get washed overboard, and since his family was on board, he wanted to make sure he and he alone was responsible for bringing the vessel through the hurricane. Many of the crew had asked him to let them spell him at the helm, but he would not hear of it. The ship's cook, knowing that he would have to at least have some hot coffee, did manage to hold the coffee pot on the stove long enough to boil the water for the coffee. That was all Captain Hassell had for three days and three nights while the hurricane lasted. But he did bring the R. H. successfully through. After the hurricane was over, they found themselves becalmed, which lasted for 25 days and my grandfather had supplies for only that period of time. On the 26th day he was down to one tin of salmon and some "hard tack," which he chose to give to the crew, and sugar water and crackers, which he gave to his family. That afternoon, around 3:00pm, a United States warship was seen approaching within a close distance and Captain Hassell put up a distress signal. The warship gave them enough supplies to get to Jacksonville, which they reached after six days. He then proceeded in finalizing the sale of the R. H. and the purchase of the orange grove, and immediately started to put the orange grove home in better shape, after which he started the trimming of the orange trees. Blossoms sprouted in a month or so, and soon tiny oranges began to appear. My mother said she had never seen him in a better frame of mind. As the oranges started to reach maturity, my grandfather envisioned a bumper crop and had by this time decided that being a "landlubber" was not so bad after all. However, his luck was about to run out, because the area was hit with one of the heaviest frosts in years and the whole crop was lost. He went bankrupt. Wasting no time, he checked in Jacksonville about possible other jobs and, as luck would have it, he found out that the Jacksonville lumber company had a three master schooner that needed a captain. He applied for the job and got it. The lumber company gave him all the information that was necessary, including the fact that he would have to run the vessel on shares of the profits, which he readily agreed to. After taking command of the vessel, his first trip was to Trinidad with a load of lumber. He took his family and dropped them off at the island of Saba, where he still owned his own home, and he continued on to Trinidad. My mother, now having reached the age of 17, had started to teach a small kindergarten class of children to help out as much as she could until her father had received his first share of the profit. Soon my Uncle Richard had reached the age of 13 and immediately went to sea as a cabin boy with an uncle of his who was captain of a 4 master square rigged ship. In the meantime, my grandfather continued to carry lumber to Trinidad and on one particular trip, after he had taken his first sight of shooting the sun, in the morning around 10 o'clock he laid down to rest. In the afternoon, just before he shot the sun again (around 3 o'clock), he called the mate and told him he was not feeling well and that he felt like he was going to die. He said, if he did, he did not want his body buried at sea, but to take tar and tar his body, wrap it in canvas, folding it over and over, and put it in the ship's hold. He gave the mate the course to steer after having taken his second shot of the sun, and found his position according to his calculation of the latitude and longitude, and that if they stayed on course as he told them, they would come to Barbados, where he wished to be buried, and so he was.

The crew then sailed the vessel to the island of Saba, where they related all the details of what had occurred. When my grandmother, Rebecca, heard it, she told my mother that six months from that date she would not be alive and let herself grieve to death. My mother then had to take over the responsibility for her younger brother Camille, who was only five years of age at the time (about 1892). After my mother reached 20 years of age (1896) she felt that she could better provide for her brother and herself by going back to New York City and with her uncle being captain of a sailing ship, he stopped at the island of Saba, packed them up, and sailed for New York. Since she knew no one in New York City, she decided after a year to go to Providence, Rhode Island, where she had relatives.

My father had fallen in love with my mother after her mother died, but she did not get to see him too often because of his going to sea. When his ship stopped at Providence, he heard from other relatives that my mother was now living there and he went to see her. They decided to marry and did so in January of the year 1902. My brother was born in December 1902. Soon after, my mother decided to go back to Saba for a short time, but that never happened, as she stayed much longer. My sister Caroline (Carry) and I were born on Saba, which is a place I can never forget, as small as it was.

As this story has been written primarily about my grandfather, I deem it to be my duty that it is centered on him. I wish to add that nothing has given me greater pleasure than to try to recall all of the information that comprises the Saga of Captain Richard Hassell.

As I was typing out this article I thought of the hundreds of Saban captains and other men of the sea who would have had similar stories which went unrecorded, and that Saba can truly be called 'Isle of a thousand sea tales.' "

Arthur Wallace Simmons

He was the youngest son of Joseph Dinzey Horton Simmons (1839-1905) and Margaret Jane Simmons Dinzey (1840-1897). His siblings were Joseph Benjamin (Blackhead Joe), Ann Louise, Lorenzo, Louise and Capt. Edwin Knight Simmons.

Capt. Arthur Wallace Simmons

He married his first cousin Mildred Simmons, a daughter of John Miller Simmons (1849-1914) and Mary Jane Simmons (1845-1917). His children were the twins Edna Mildred and Ethel Marguerite, Alma Louise, Edgar Arthur, Olga May and the youngest of all, Viola Adele. He obtained his US citizenship on April 5, 1901, Southern District Court of New York.

He was a Sea Captain on tall sailing ships, one of them was the four-masted schooner 'Margaret Throop', 1264 tons, built by Dunn and Elliot in Thomaston in 1918, and belonged to John Elliot & Co. of New York. He lost that ship in the 1920's and thereafter was on steamships.

He was 5' 10", had blue eyes and reddish gold hair. His nickname was 'Pappy'. Sometimes, his youngest daughter Viola would stay with him when he was prepping the ship for its next voyage. He would make a swing with boards and ropes from the boom of the mizenmast and she would swing out over the sea. When she spent the night over on the ship, Capt. Simmons would tuck her in a small sofa placed against the wall to avoid her from falling out.

Replica of the Schooner 'Margaret Throop' built by John William Curry

Usually these large ships would go for long trips so it was not surprising that the captains would bring along their families. On schooners such as the Margaret Throop, the structure of the crew would vary. There were Mates (two, sometimes three), a boatswain, a carpenter, sometimes a sail-maker, a number of able-bodied seamen, and a cook. Family lore tells a story about the cook on the Margaret Throop was shooting rats. That did not amuse the Captain!

Hard work was characteristic on these large schooners, however when a vessel was becalmed, the crew members could go fishing. Fresh fish was always a welcome substitute to the cured meat usually served onboard. Some cooks were better than others, and some downright awful. The cook prepared three meals a day, kept the galley clean, did not stand watch, and unlike the rest of the crew, could sleep all night. Only when there was a call of "all hands" he was expected to work on deck or aloft. Still the cooks work was a challenging one, particularly in severe weather.

Ship manifest of October 16, 1918 shows Arthur Wallace Simmons arriving at New York from Rio de Janiero as the master of the Schooner "E Starr Jones" which was built in 1904. She was 185 feet long and 38 feet wide. In 1918 Arthur Wallace Simmons surrendered her license when she was stranded on Rio Grande do Sul Bar, Brazil.

He lived with his family at 100 Rodgus Ave., Brooklyn, NY; also 1307 St. John's Place, Brooklyn, NY. His niece Ann Louisa Simmons gave an address of 1829 or 1259 St. John's Place, Brooklyn, NY upon her arrival on the SS San Juan on June 6, 1927. By the Census of 1930 they live at 223 Schenectady Ave, Brooklyn NY.

The last ship he was on was the "Flomar", owned by the Calmer Steamship Co. of NY.

He died on August 14th 1934 and is interred at Cypress Hill Cemetery, Lot Number 15787 B20.

William Rudolph 'Chila' Dinzey

William Rudolph Dinzey also known as 'Chila' from The Bottom was born on Oct 11th 1876 to Johanna 'Hanna' Dinzey. He had two siblings: Gertrude and Fedor Dinzey.

He was the Captain of the Boatmen at Fort Bay, who in former times and many years brought goods and people safely to shore from larger ships arriving Saba. He was followed by William James 'Jimma' Heyliger and his sons Nederville Heyliger and Carlton Heyliger. This was a responsible position as it required much skill and responsibility in bringing passengers and cargo to shore at Fort Bay or Ladder Bay.

The Captain had to count the waves and make the decision when to give the order to row full speed towards the shore before the next wave caught up with you and swamped the boat. Sometimes the captain would wait outside the breakers for what seemed forever and then suddenly would shout out the command "Take her now!" or something of the sorts. As a passenger your greatest concern was to make it to the rocky shore safely and out of the boat as quick as possible. On the shore part of the crew would be there in the water waiting to catch the boat and haul her up beyond the breakers as soon as possible. The more agile passengers would sometimes jump out and assist with pulling up the heavy boat as far as possible.

Recovering an Electric Generator which fell overboard as it was landed

Most of the times they were successful in their task of moving goods and people from and to the vessels. However, one incident which made news was when the Saba Electric Company N.V. brought in its first 300 kw diesel engine from New York. Elmer Linzey and his aunt Mrs. Othella Edwards owned the company and Elmer had accompanied the engine all the way from New York via several islands and then had the engine transferred on Curacao to the monthly steamer the M.V. "Antilia and in the process of landing the engine at Saba it fell overboard into the sea. But nothing could deter the Sabans. They dove down strapped the engine with ropes and everyone who could pull showed up and dragged the engine onto the shore. That same engine was cleaned up and went on to do its part of delivering energy to Saba for the next thirty years.

'Chila' never married nor had any children. He died on July 26th 1963.

Anthony Dudley Granger

Anthony was the second child born to Anthony Granger and Jessarial Lynch (1879-1958), born on March 21st 1905. His siblings were: Walter Maurine, Daniel, Ernest, Elizabeth Hall, Peter Leicester 'Sessy', George Clifton, James Lodvey and Carl Ambrose Granger.

He worked for Lago Shipping Co. as an Apprentice Fireman, on the oil tanker Oranjestad.

As many seaman in the war era, he died on February 16th, 1942 when the ship was torpedoed and sunk by German U-boat (U-156), at anchor near San Nicolas, Aruba

Eric Norbert Linzey

Was the son of Joseph Evan Linzey and Geraldine Barnes, born in the village of St. John's, Saba on April 7th 1923. He had a sister, Annie Vincentia Linzey.

He worked as a Steward, aboard the oil tanker SS Oranjestad, Lago Shipping Co.

On February 16th 1942 his ship was torpedoed and sunk by German submarine U-boat (U-156), and died a seaman's death at anchor near San Nicolas, Aruba.

Darcy Kenneth Lynch

He was one of the children of Charles Josephus Lynch and Rebecca Zagers, born December 25th 1909. His siblings were Edith, Vandeline Rose, Maude Vernice, Paul Cedron, Olaf Henry, and Ursulita Lynch. Aldo, half-brother of Helen Louise Lynch. He married Ulrica Hassell (1905-1988) and had three children: Winifred Marguerite, Emmanuel Arturo and Clinton Stevanis Lynch.

He worked as a Sailor aboard the tanker SS Oranjestad, property of Lago Shipping Co.

He died on February 16th 1942 when the ship was torpedoed and sunk by German U-boat (U-156), at anchor near San Nicolas, Aruba.

James Andrew Maxwell

Jim was the youngest son of Sophia Maxwell (1883-1945), and was born January 6th 1913. His siblings were Arthur Monroe and James Eric Maxwell.

He was a Sailor aboard the oil tanker SS Punta Gorda, Lago Shipping Co.

He died on September 18th 1944 in a lights-out and radio silence situation because of the presence of U-boats in the area, when the ship he was traveling in collided with Belgian tanker Ampetco II, about 5 miles out of Cabo San Roman (Falcon, Venezuela).

Carl Aloysius Simmons

Carl was a son of Jacob Thomson Simmons (1885-1951) and his second wife Felicita Dinzey (1891-1947); he was born on February 10th 1910, and was followed by his siblings Felicita Eulalie, Annie Louise, Jacob Thomson Allewer and Hubert MacDonald Simmons. He was also a half-brother of Beatrix Ann Simmons.

He worked as a Steward aboard the oil tanker Ferncastle, property of A/S Glitre, Oslo (Norway)

He died in the Indian Ocean, on July 12th 1943 in a lifeboat, after surviving the sinking of his ship by the German Auxiliary Cruiser "Michel".

Clifford Achilles Wilson

He was born on August 5th 1910 as a son of Jane Wilson. His sibling was Adam Wilson.

Clifford was a fireman on the oil tanker Oranjestad, property of the Lago Shipping Co.

Died on 16 February 1942, when ship was torpedoed and sunk by German U-boat (U-156), anchored at port near San Nicolas, Aruba.

John Wilson

Son of Ophelia Wilson (1883-1972), he was born on July 24th 1913 at The Bottom, Saba. His siblings were: William Jackson, Moses, Richard, Constantia Blanche and Joseph Wilson.

He was a fireman on the oil tanker Tia Juana, property of Lago Shipping Co.

He died on February 16th 1942 when the ship SS Tia Juana was torpedoed and sunk by German U-boat (U-502), in the Gulf of Venezuela.

Thomas Simmons

Commodore Thomas Simmons

He was the fourth son of Joseph Benjamin "Black Head Joe" Simmons (1866-1934) and Margaret Jane "Maggie Jane" Simmons (1869-1952) who had a large family of ten children. Maggie Jane was born in New York. Her mother was a Manning from Barbados and died at a young age in New York. Her father, George Anthony Simmons, brought Maggie back to Saba for his mother (Mary Elizabeth Zagers) to raise her. As in so many cases back then George was lost in 1876 on a schooner in the North Atlantic. When Maggie Jane was an old woman, her son Captain Thomas Simmons took her back to New York where she lived out her final days and was buried. Maggie Jane had ten children, several of whom died at sea. In the back of the Anglican Church in The Bottom there is a plaque which reads as follows:

> *"In loving memory of John Simmons, age 52 years. David W. Simmons, age 40 years, Richard R. Simmons, age 22 years, Isaac Simmons age 16 years. Lost at sea, September 1918. We cannot Lord, thy purpose see; but all is well that's done by thee."*

John Simmons was captain of a Danish registered schooner from St. Thomas. The vessel and its crew were lost coming out of Miami. Richard 22 and Isaac 16 were sons of Maggie Jane.

Captain 'Tom', as he was fondly called, worked his way up from a cabin-boy on schooners plying the West Indian trade to 'Commodore' of the Moore-McCormick line. He sailed as a deck boy on schooners trading out of New York, Boston and the Gulf and Caribbean ports, making second mate in 1914.

The longest time he had at sea was in 1914 when he spent 119 days aboard a four-masted schooner sailing from the Gulf port of Mississippi to Buenos Aires, Argentina, with a cargo of lumber.

Immediately after he had passed his examination at the Custom House, and received his Master's Certificate, about 10:00am, he went down two flights in the building and put his name on the list as available for a ship. And about 2:00pm that same afternoon he got a ship assigned and sailed the next day. His first ship was the SS Hegira, which was to sail from Galveston to Germany. Tommy boarded the train for Galveston that same day and was on his way to his command.

Captain Simmons spent sixteen years with the Munson Line before going to Moore-McCormack. He joined Munson in 1922 as third officer of the Munrio, became chief officer, then commanded several of the Munson ships, including the Pan America, Munargo, Western World, American Legion and Southern Cross.

Captain Simmons went to Moore-McCormack in 1938 when the Good Neighbor Fleet was organized to operate between New York and the east coast of South America. He was given command of the Argentina which he commanded ever since, including the years of the war.

The old "Argentina", under his command, was refitted as a transport ship and was the first troop ship to enter the ports of Australia during World War II and was on standby for D-Day, stationed in England. He later became the first commodore of the Moore McCormick Line in 1958. He spent fifty-two years at sea, traveled over 6 million miles over the seven seas beginning in 1911, three years after he left his beloved Saba, and was awarded with the National Order of the Southern Cross in 1963, the highest state honor to a foreigner by the government of Brazil.

The following article is taken from the Brazil Herald of February 24th 1963:

RETIRING COMMODORE SIMMONS RECEIVES BRAZILIAN DECORATION

Rio de Janeiro – Commodore Thomas N. Simmons, who arrives tomorrow in Rio on his last cruise aboard the Moore McCormack liner 'Argentina', yesterday was awarded the Cruzeiro do Sul by the Government of Brazil. He received Brazil's highest award given to citizens of foreign countries in ceremonies during the ship's stopover in Salvador, Bahia, from the hands of Bahia Governor Juracy Magalhaes. Commodore Simmons, friend and councilor to a myriad of international travelers, culminates 50 years on the sea on the SS Argentina's current "Sea Safari" cruise. This 63 day trip is Commodore Simmons' last, as he has announced his retirement effective upon his return, April 17. And coincidentally another 50 years are celebrated in 1963 – the 50th anniversary of Moore McCormack Lines, founded in 1913 – one of America's foremost steamship owners and operators, whose fleet includes the two new passenger liners, "Argentina" and 'Brazil", and 42 modern cargo liners.

The innate modesty of the Commodore camouflages a colorful career. To him all the flavor and excitement of the sea is not commonplace – far from it- but so much a part of his life that he accepts the unusual as the everyday, the crisis as the normal. The highlight of his career are people he knew and knows and loves; the Duke of Windsor, Clark Gable, Bing Crosby, corporate Presidents, Cardinals, Artists, Singers. Summing up, all are Tom Simmons' exciting moments. The Commodore was born on Saba Island in the West Indies, of Dutch forefathers of seafaring bent. Commodore Simmons' last trip takes him amidst friends in the Caribbean ports of Barbados, in Brazil, Uruguay and Argentina.

Thence he and the "Argentina" sail to South and East Africa, through the Suez, to the Mediterranean and homeward via Italy, Spain and Portugal. These are familiar friendly places to Tom Simmons, faces of friends whom he relishes visiting. At many of the ports, officials, old cronies, visiting traveling companions and the Simmons people are planning commemorative ceremonies marking the 50th and retirement year of service of Commodore Thomas N. Simmons. A Grandfather a dozen times over, Commodore Simmons enjoys his holidays at his home on Long Island. But the sea is part of him, and anyone can see from his "Argentina" that he is a man of the sea."

A side note about his middle initial in this press note. The "N" was not for Norman as many people became to believe. As a matter of fact, he had no middle name. Family lore indicates that when they were filling out the enlistment forms the clerk typed "NN" to signify "None / No Name" as was customary at the time. Somehow, this was translated over the years to be an abbreviation of "Norman."

He was born on April 4th, 1895. He met his wife Enid May Simmons (1902-1990) in New York (she was born Montego Bay, Jamaica in 1902). She was a daughter of Captain Solomon "Butchy Coonks" Simmons also of Saba and her mother was the daughter of the Scottish Customs collector there.

He also had the privilege and honor of bringing the GI Brides of World War II to the United States. The *SS Argentina* was getting prepared to journey to France to pick up U.S. troops. At the last moment, the ship was ordered to sail for Southampton, England, where they would pick up English women who had married American soldiers during the War, and take them to New York City.

A total of 452 brides, 30 of them pregnant, 173 children, and one war groom boarded the *SS Argentina* at Southampton on the afternoon of January 26, 1946. The voyage was safe and pleasant with all the attention of most of the crew on the war brides who were enjoying amenities such as fresh bread, marmalade and jams, steaks and other items such as fresh fruit for the first time in many years, as they were all too scarce during war time. Overall it was a safe trip, even though it was pretty rough at times with heavy seas washing the decks.

Thomas Simmons signals for the last time 'Finished with Engines' on his retirement trip

Commodore Thomas Simmons had radioed ahead to "someone of importance in New York" and said that it would be nice if the Statue of Liberty was lit up during the morning of their arrival to United States. The first sight of America was at 2:30 a.m., February 4th, 1946, and they all lined the rail to see Lady Liberty which was lit up for their arrival. The bright lights of New York highlighted a beautiful memory of a grand welcome to them.

The Statue was lit that night for the first time since World War II and as the brides arrived in the early morning hours, they saw the Lady in all her full glory. This was a wonderful sight for the brides since they had been living in blackout for so many years. The Argentina finally docked in New York City, Pier 54 Hudson River.

The tall 68-year-old mariner took his last salute on the gangway of the luxury liner, S.S. Argentina, which he brought into Pier 97 after a 63-day cruise. Most of the officers and crew on deck who came to see him leave looked down at their shoes or turned their heads away, as though they were looking at something far off.

Within the next few weeks, he and his wife 'May' moved from their home in Manhasset, Long Island, to Ft. Lauderdale, FL, where they built a house not too far from deep-sea fishing docks that Captain Simmons knew well and enjoyed during his retirement. He died at the ripe age of 74 on March 20th 1970.

George Bernard Johnson

George Bernard (aka Leonard) was the eighth child born to Daniel Jacobus Johnson and Marie Elizabeth Johnson. He was born on March 22, 1909 at Hell's Gate and his siblings were Dulcie Claudine, Silvia Otilia, Pauline Gonzales, Marie Lonisee, Mildred, Corine (Cora), Daniel Thomas, Sebastian and May Johnson.

As many Sabans, George found work on the large oil tankers of the oil industry in Aruba. A sailor around the world for more than forty years, he was part of the crew on a tanker in the bombing of Japan shortly after Pearl Harbor. They were sitting ducks as the destroyers had moved off during the bombing of Tokyo, but he survived that and many more adventures at sea. When asked of all the countries he had visited if he had a favorite, without hesitation he would say Cuba. He worked on a tanker which supplied fuel to different ports there and he had nothing but praise for the old Cuban people.

In June 1934, he married Erla Hyacinth Hassell, a daughter of Thomas Mardenborough Hassell (1877-1954) and Ann Elizabeth Dowling (1877-1958). They had six children: George Bernard Jr., Leonard 'Lenny', Erla Hyacinth, Arthur Garvice, Henry 'Dutch' and Brian.

He died at the age of 72 on Jan 16 1982 on Saba at Windwardside.

Herbert Lockland Heyliger

Was born into a large family; he was the fourth child born to John Joseph Dinzey Heyliger and Mary Ann 'Sis' Simmons. He was born on Saba on June 24, 1868. His siblings were: Engle, Ada, Laura Augusta, Theodore Sidgismund 'Mr. Dory', Florence Constantia 'Florrie', Arnold Washington, Marie and Alaric.

He was married to Amy Simmons, a daughter of Edmund Rudolph Simmons and Ann Posie 'Tanta' Simmons, and had four children: Amy Beatrice, Edith Evelyn, Louise, and Herbert Lisle Heyliger.

Herbert is listed as the Captain of the Margaret Throop, a 1264 ton schooner, built by Dunn and Elliot in Thomaston in 1918. He arrived in New York on May 23, 1919 sailing back from Genoa, Italy; also, part of the crew was his brother Theodore S. Heyliger (Engineer) and Cameron Simmons (Chief Mate).

Arrives in 1893 aboard barkentine "Gem". He immigrated in 1894 and is naturalized in the 1910 Census; they live at 792 Park Place Brooklyn NY.

In 1920 he was listed as the Master of the Panamanian flag sailing vessel, "Reine Marie Stuart." The ship of 1087 Tons, was a four-masted barkentine built in 1919 by Richard, Arthur and Frank Elliot of the Dunn and Elliot Company as a coal carrier. She was the last large vessel to hail from Thomaston, ME and the last barkentine built on the Maine coast.

He was also Captain of large sail ships such as the four-masted schooners "E. Marie Brown" and the "East Star Jones", as well as the five-masted schooner "Rebecca Palmer."

He is listed as living at several locations in New York: at 792 Park Pl, Brooklyn NY (1910 Census), 2316 Newkirk Ave., Brooklyn, NY (1920 Census), and at 1222 East 2 Ave, Booklyn, NY (1930 Census).

Cohone Johnson

He was the fourth child born to Richard Cohone Johnson (1806-1882) and his wife Mary Catherine Hassell; his siblings were Peter James, Mary Catherine, Rebecca, Richard, Elizabeth and Susanna Johnson. On May 3rd 1876 he married Elizabeth 'Betsy' Hassell (1851-1900), a daughter of Edward Hassell and Mary Johnson.

On Saba, when a hurricane was coming, our forefathers went by instinct following closely signs given by the animals and how they behaved. Frequent small showers coming in, the sea getting rougher, and the skies darker were clear signs of the potential rough time ahead. At the time Saba was very much dependent on its schooners owned by local people.

We were fortunate to come across an account written by Richard Austin Johnson about a hurricane of 1871 and his grandfather Cohone having to leave his family behind to go and take a schooner anchored at Fort Bay out to sea to weather the storm.

"The last day of September 1871, a day long to be remembered by the inhabitants of Saba, broke with an overcast-sky and a light drizzle. Mountainous easterly ground-swells pounded the coast line, throwing spume in the air to be blown away by the increasing Northeast winds.

My grandfather, Cohone Johnson, was awake at daybreak and for a while listened to the roar of the waves 15 hundred feet below, then hastily dressing himself, he went outside and noted with a seaman's eye, the signs which clearly heralded an approaching hurricane.

A schooner at sea, similar to the one in this story

Going back inside the house he wakened his wife Betsy and said, "I don't want to alarm you, Betsy, but I believe a hurricane is coming; see to it that the children are dressed and fed, while I secure the loose things and batten down some of the windows.

At the time, Cohone was sailing a two-masted 90 foot vessel, which was at anchor in the Ladder Bay.

Her owner, and captain, was at home, recuperating from a severe grippe and in no fit condition to take the vessel to sea. Cohone's mind turned to the vessel as he worked and wondered what old Captain Richard Simmons would decide to do. At that moment my grandfather had no premonition, that before the day ended, he would be fighting for his life, on a sea gone mad with hurricane force winds.

As the morning wore on, Cohone's neighbors, came to him for advice about the weather. To one and all he said "Prepare for a hurricane, which I expect to reach us before nightfall".

About 10 o'clock, a boy, breathless from running, came to Cohone with a message from Capt. Simmons, saying "There is a hurricane approaching and I need you to help take the vessel to sea. Come at once." After instructing his wife to have one of her cousins' stay with her during the hurricane, Cohone took leave of his family and raced to the Ladder Bay, where a rowboat was waiting to take him to the ship. After being nearly swamped because of the increasing wind and sea, Cohone managed to board the vessel, where he found to his dismay that only the captain, the mate, a cabin boy and himself were aboard.

Going to the cabin, Cohone confronted the captain, who sat at the cabin table, reading the Bible and demanded to know why he had been sent for and none of the other sailors.

With tears in his eyes, Captain Simmons said "The cowards refused to leave home. Just plain scared to risk their lives in a hurricane at sea. Pointing to the mate, who was snoring in his bunk, with a half empty bottle of rum at his side", he said. "Just look at that drunken slob there. Don't expect any help from him. If I come out of this alive it will be my pleasure to kick him off my vessel. Now I just don't know what to do."

The schooner "Dorothy Palmer" in rough seas. Our Saban ancestors who survived these storms had many tales to pass on to their descendants.

Cohone thought for a minute and said "Captain, we cannot abandon the ship, even if we wanted to because we cannot get back to the shore. If we stay here any longer and the wind moves farther north, this will be open harbor and then nothing can save us. I suggest that we slip the anchor hoist the staysail and run south." Then he added as an afterthought; "but we need your help at the wheel, until we can get the vessel underway." To this plan the Captain agreed. Going on deck he said to the cabin boy, a sturdy youth of sixteen years, "Boy, you and I are the only ones to get this vessel under way. I want you to begin hoisting the staysail when I give you the word. Can I depend on you?" The boy nodded wordlessly. Cohone went forward, unshackled the chain and said to the cabin boy, "Now stand to hoist away." Looking aft he saw that the Captain was at the wheel. Waiting until the vessels bow swung to port, he yelled "Now!" and released the anchor chain, which went out of the hosepipe with a roar and was gone. Leaping to the assistance of the cabin boy, they hoisted the staysail. The vessel released from her anchor surged forward, driven by a wind that had increased to gale-force.

The Captain was glad to have Cohone relieve him at the wheel because he was a sick man and had the chills, brought on by the wind-driven rain.

All afternoon and far into the night, the vessel fled Southward, driven by the wind which had increased to hurricane force, while Cohone fought the wheel to keep her on course. Shortly before midnight the cabin boy, who acted as lookout, yelled "Breakers on the port bow." Cohone immediately, heaved on the wheel swinging the vessel's bow away and to starboard. Shortly afterward, during a lightning flash, Cohone saw that they had narrowly missed piling-up on Isla de Aves, also known as Bird Island, which is situated about 110 miles South and West of Montserrat.

About one hour later, the wind veered to the South. Cohone again changed course and fled before the wind. It was shortly after this that a mountainous wave loomed up amidships on the vessels starboard side. Yelling to the Cabin boy to jump for the riggings, Cohone let go of the wheel and did the same. With a thunderous roar the wave crashed down on the vessel, smothering her under tons of water and heaving her over on her beam ends. There she stayed until Cohone jumped to the deck in knee-deep water and seizing an axe, chopped away part of the bulwark, allowing the water to pour off. Slowly the vessel came back to even keel. Both the galley and the ships boat had vanished in the darkness.

During the early morning hours, the wind, which was now blowing from the South-Southwest, lessened and the sky, began clearing. The island of Santa Cruz could now be seen ahead. Cohone again changed course, this time to Eastward. On the day after the hurricane, which was afterwards known as the Great Storm, Cohone dropped anchor at the Ladder Bay. The island that Cohone had left the day before was devastated, but luckily for my Grandfather, both he and his family were very much alive."

George Irvin Holm

George Irvin Holm (1891-1984). His father died in an accident with a falling stone under the cliffs at Crispeen when the Captain was only twelve years old and his brother Ralph, almost nine. He started sailing at age 13 as Cabin Boy on a two-masted schooner '*Mary Love*', which belonged to Captain Ben Hassell and Captain Lovelock Hassell (Ben's father-in-law).

In 1906 he visited the United States for the first time. The '*Mary Love*' took 22 passengers from Saba, Statia and St. Maarten and brought back the lumber to build the home of Captain Ernest Alfred Johnson on Booby Hill. In 1909 he moved to New York and started to work on sailing ships and yachts. At the age of 18, he sailed as a 'donkeyman[5]' on the '*Prescot Palmer*' sister ship to the five-masted '*Rebecca Palmer*'. Another large 5-masted sail vessel he worked on was the SV "Governor Brooks," on which he as a donkey-man.

---

[5] A crew member whose job is to deal with the operation and maintenance of any and all assorted machinery other than the ship's main engines. Usually reports to the Second-Engineer.

He obtained his Third-Mate license in 1916, in 1917 his 2rd-Mate license and by 1918 he became a Chief Mate, and joined the US Navy as Lieutenant sailing on a troopship to Liverpool, England. He was transferred and worked as an assistant to the port captain of Brest, France, then to a navy ship with Headquarters at Cardiff, England. He worked on the E.M. Elridge, a four masted schooner, as Second-Mate.

He enlisted for WW I when he was working on the SS Owego as the Third-Mate.

After the war he became captain of a private yacht named 'Halcyon' which later became a rum-runner. In 1931 he became captain of a steamer for the DuPont's (International Trading Co.), then went over to Prudential Lines as captain and remained with them until he retired. The ship was the "Thomas E. Mitchell" and it was used on the South American run.

He was also the Chief-Mate of the SS Edith owned by the Bull Insular Lined which plied the Caribbean islands, in particular Puerto Rico, with some Saban hands onboard.

Captain Holm died at the age of 93. His remains were brought back to Saba, and a lifelong wish was fulfilled when he was laid to rest next to the grave of his beloved father. His last years of retirement had been spent partly on Saba and he was very helpful to Will Johnson, the politician, historian, and author in verifying much of the material contained in his books.

The schooner '*Wyoming*' was the largest wooden schooner ever built. She was a six-masted schooner designed by Bant Hanson of Bath, Maine. She was proudly launched on Wednesday December 15, 1909 by the firm of Percy & Small in Bath, Maine. Ralph Hassell was a 'donkeyman' on this schooner and Capt. Irvin Holm also sailed on her as a mate, as told Will Johnson in his interviews of the amount of work involved in working on one of these large schooners. Other sailors who worked the Wyoming were Simon Hassell and Edward Johnson.

While at sea, donkey engines could be used to operate the anchor windlass and bilge pumps. He could also be called on to perform the duties of fireman or greaser. And from what I can find, it was not unusual for the donkeyman to do watch duties. A "jack of all trades" as one might say. On some ships the "Donkey engine/boiler" could be used to supply emergency propulsion. Running steam engines was a dangerous job and that is where his real knowledge and skills was of great importance, even though there was down time while at sea.

The Donkeyman was the equivalent of the Bosun on deck; he was in charge of the greasers, donkey/greasers, firemen, engine room boys. He mainly answered to the second engineer. His principle duties were to supervise and take the burden off the second engineer, regarding maintenance, painting, cleaning and before engine room store-keepers, he would do the stores ordering and distribution.

In January 1943 the *SS William Wirt* was subjected to four separate enemy bombing attacks while in convoy in the Mediterranean. It was the first experience for many: of the seamen stationed with the gun crews but they served like seasoned veterans. Several planes were shot down and many others damaged or dispelled. This excellent performance was largely due to the skillful training and indoctrination given by the Master, and Chief Mate George Irvin Holms who were also responsible for the high morale in the ship's company. Holms also helped the Master in maneuvering the ship to keep a maximum number of guns bearing on the planes. [Holmes resided in Richmond Hill, NY] July 12, 1946

William Thomas Hassell

He was the first born child of William Hassell (1870-xxxx) and Vanetia Simmons (1874-1920), born on January 17th 1897. His siblings were Robert, Benjamin, Mary Ann and Georgina Hyacinth.

He enlisted as a Seaman in 1918 for WW I; at the time he was working for the Federal Steamship Line out of New York, NY where he used the 27 South St of Mr. Kaliski as his address, and for any correspondence to his father, William Hassell. He married to Ina Hassell, a daughter of Peter John Hassell (1856-1915) and Ann Catherine Dowling (1871-1935), on February 27th 1922.

Waldron Hassell

The youngest son of Capt. Henry Johnson Hassell (1854-1957) and Sarah Ellen Johnson (1857-xxxx) was born November 17th 1895 on Saba. His siblings were: Mildred, Eleanor, Mary, Annie, Georgiana, Mildred, Henry, Violet and Vaneta.

He enlisted as a Seaman in WW I. He never married nor had children.

Alexander Heyliger

He was born to Catharine Heyliger on February 14th 1863, at The Bottom. He married Sylvania Rock, a daughter of Sophie Rock, on November 28th 1888, on The Bottom, Saba. Their marriage was blessed with six children, although only four survived: Frederick Williams, Romalia, Alma Odlin, Alexander Harris, Frank Ashton and the youngest Edward Clinton.

Like very few, Alexander Heyliger was a sturdy seaman but also what we could call a "jack of all trades"; he not only built his own schooner with his very own hands, with help from his father Gideon Godet Heyliger, out of the timber wood from the ancient Mahogany trees in the rain-forest high-up on Mt. Scenery. A feat nothing short than truly remarkable! Think of the level of difficulty for each stage! To harvest the wood from high in the rainforest, preparing the wood for construction, the construction itself, launching and sailing your own schooner! A tribute to man's determination and ingenuity no less!

He also used the ship in his trade. Hence, he was respectfully referred to thereafter as "Capt'n Alex" -- though not officially commissioned, he certainly had proven his seamanship as a true son of Saba, in the days "When the ships were made of wood, and the men were made of iron!"

He named the ship "Thelma"; she was a long, sleek, black schooner (from the mahogany wood) and she rode low and sailed silent and swift through the water. The perfect smuggling schooner, used to trade goods and contraband throughout the West Indies. No doubt making credit to their pirate ancestry! Rum was the order of the day, and the Cove of Rum Bay on Saba was safe for transferring. He also ran sulphur and mercury from the mine on Saba. After moving to Long Island, Alexander continued to receive pure mercury from Saba, smuggled through the US mail in a dried-fruit box with a false bottom, by his son Frederik.

It is also said in family lore that his daughter Romalia, who moved to the States with her husband Joseph Woods, ran horse-racing numbers quietly from her Long Island home for, and protected by, the local Italian mafia, for decades. Sweet Romalia was a bookie for the mob!

Alexander Heyliger died on May 21st 1931 at The Bottom.

Walter Allen Whitfield

He was the oldest son of Maraja Winfield/Whitfield, born on August 10th 1912 at the Bottom. His siblings were Maud Stella, John and Ernest Lisle Whitfield.

He worked under contract with the Lago Shipping Co. aboard the oil tanker Tia Juana as a Fireman.

He died the night of February 16th 1942 when his ship was torpedoed and sunk by German U-boat (U-502), in the Gulf of Venezuela.

As the publication of this book, we have not uncovered if he had any family.

Stanley Hassell

A retired US Coast Guard, Chief Mate Stanley Hassell was a son of Richard Hassell and Judith Ann Hassell (1868-1918). Born on Saba on January 13 1898, his siblings were Evan, Gladys, Elsie Beatrice, John Ellis and Nina Marguerite Hassell. About 1919 he married a Scottish girl named Charlotte Murray and had two children: Douglas and Richard Hassell.

He worked as a Quartermaster during WW I on the USACS United States Army Courier Service "The Floridian." He was a Chief Mate for the US Coast Guard. He died in Providence, RI on 23rd December 1948.

William James 'Jimma' Heyliger

He was the third child born to the couple of Gideon Godet 'Giddy' Heyliger (1843-1915) and Mary Every (1845-1926). 'Jimma' was born on Saba the 23rd of September of 1870. His siblings were Eldecia, Lawrence 'Lalie', Gideon Godet, Theodore, Edica, Thomas, Mary Susan and Virginia Heyliger.

William James Heyliger 'Jimma' was for many years Captain of the boatmen who landed cargo from the sloops and schooners of former times, and he in turn took over from William 'Chila' Dinzey.

He married twice; first he married Helen Heyliger on February 12th 1896, with whom he had nine children: Viola, Winifred, Kenneth, James Alfred, Catherine, Olivine, Carlton Owen, Nederville and William Cedric. He married the second time to Lilly Irene Collins on April 12th 1967 and he had two additional children: Brontie Beatrix and James Allicks Heyliger.

He died on November 30th 1969.

Augustus 'Gustus' Whitfield

He was the third son of Cato Whitfield and Ann Exeria 'Nanny' Blijden (1868-1963). His siblings were Alexander, Cato Jr., Ether Ellen and Hilton Whitfield.

His first navigation job was with his father Cato Whitfield who was a Mate on a schooner trading from Barbados to France. On a trip Gustus became ill and was dropped off in Bermuda with intentions to go back to Saba via St. Kitts, where he died about 1914.

Hilton Whitfield

As reflected in an interview by Dr. Julia Crane in her book "Saba Silhouettes", one can envision Hilton as a man who was the 'salt of the earth'. A real nice guy, whom was keen on making himself perfectly clear; when he spoke, as he had the custom to always repeat everything twice. Hilton was married to the aunt of Prime Minister Maria Liberia Peters however he did not have any children by her. Nevertheless, before he married in 1946, he had three love children: Stella Harriet Jones, Claudia Whitfield and Joseph Aloysious 'Josie' Woods.

Hilton Whitfield with his daughters Claudia and Stella

He was the fifth and youngest son of Cato Whitfield and Ann Exeria 'Nanny' Blijden (1868-1963). His siblings were Alexander, Cato Jr., Augustus 'Gustus' and Ether Ellen Whitfield.

His first incursions to the sea were under the tutelage of Capt. Thomas Charles Vanterpool. He studied at the Saba Navigation School but his studies were cut half-way when the instructor, Freddie Simmons, died. He was able to convince Capt. Vanterpool to take him as a mess boy at the age of 19; although he knew he was a little old to be in that position, he was determined to learn quickly the real seaman-skills he would need to progress from wooden sloops and schooners to the large (and profitable) steamers. Before that, he tended to the animals, farmed and helped at home providing fish he would catch.

He became a good hand and served on some important schooners of the day which usually traded on Curacao, Barbados, Sint Maarten, St. Kitts, Demerara and so on, transporting people and goods: the Ina Marie (Capt. Vanterpool), the Three Sisters (Capt. Will Leverock), Diamond Ruby, the Vivian P. Smith and a the sloop Nautilius property of Phyllis Randolph Dunkin were some of the vessels he navigated. The latter was involved in an accident which resulted in her loss and put in danger the lives of its crew: Randolph Dunkin, his brother Garnet Hughes, William James 'Jamesie' Linzey and Hilton Whitfield. The ship headed out into the dark; while between Statia and St. Kitts it got tripped over by the wind-whipped, white-capped Caribbean Sea. All hands were saved.

He finally got his big break in 1930 with a recommendation from one of his sailor mates and landed a job on a Shell Oil Tanker in Curacao. He received an invitation in 1935 from his brother to join him in Aruba where he got a job on ESSO Tankers working the refinery where he worked for a stint of twelve years aboard the Lake Tanker Hooiberg servicing Lake Maracaibo. These ships would sail out of the port of St. Nicholas with their lowest deck at four to six feet above the water and return with the same decks awash, burdened with some 40,000 barrels of Venezuelan Mara crude oil for the Lago Refinery, the largest in the world at its time. Over his nineteen years on tankers he worked on: *Carapeter*, *ESSO Panama*, *Cumarebo* and the *Hooiberg*, just to mention a few.

During WW II he was a witness to several tankers go under attack of U-Boats and be lost: the *Oranjestad*, the *Pedernales* and a gulf boat named *Manacus*. Also the *Tewana* and the San Nicolas coming out of Lake Maracaibo.

After 1954 he came home to rest. He eventually moved to Europe working for the Reynolds Aluminum Co. working on the bauxite trade between Haiti, Jamaica, Corpus Christi and Mobile. As result of an accident in 1958 he was injured on his wrists which affected his working skills on ships. He came home and did some fishing until he landed a job with the government working the phone switchboard.

On his time off he mostly enjoyed catching turtles with nets, fishing for moonfish, wahoo and red fish; hunting for wild goat and pigeons, with his friends Carlton Heyliger, James Linzey, Wathey Woods and Peter Linzey. Hilton would build his own nets as well as his fishing pods.

Ralph Holm

Helen & Ralph Holm

Ralph Holm, born October 2nd, 1894, the son of George William Holm (1862-1903) and Elderina Hassell (1871-xxxx), was a brother of Capt. George Irvin Holm. Other siblings were Josiah and Ethel Holm. He began sailing at age 15 with Captain Lovelock Hassell on the *'Peerless'*, a two-masted schooner.

In 1911, he went to the United States where he worked on tugboats and yachts. He became Captain of a yacht for *'Farrell Line'*. Then he became

Mate on a ship which was torpedoed during World War I off Trinidad. He drifted around in a lifeboat until he was rescued. He was also shipwrecked on a coal-boat with Captain Harold Simmons of The Bottom. The boat sank on route from Philadelphia to Boston, all were saved. He then began working as Captain of steamships for Farrell Lines until his retirement in 1946. He used to sail mostly to Europe, and took part in D-Day and went into the beach with his ship. His wife was Helen Johnson of Sint Eustatius. He never had any children and died on April 8, 1976 in St. Petersburg, Pinellas Co., FL.

Leo Alphons Ignatius Chance

Leo A.I. Chance was born on Saba November 8th, 1932 to Bertin Chance and Louisa Maybeline 'May' Elcock Rollock. He was largely formed by his Saba upbringing, although his parents were not from Saba. A young boy back in those days had a shared responsibility in the family survival and thus hard and sustained work was the order of the day. Growing up on Saba as part of a large family back in the nineteen-thirties and forties was not easy, especially in those years of World War II. He had to work hard along with his father who was a carpenter, a merchant and Island Trader, and also a planter.

After completing elementary school he continued his education on St. Maarten. His love for politics started early on. He got in trouble with the Roman Catholic nuns because of this. The nuns were supporting the NVP party, which was then considered partial to the Roman Catholic

Church. At the age of 18 Leo made a rousing speech on the Square in favor of the Democratic Party. The crowd liked his speech too much for the nuns' taste and it cost him some points at school.

Later he started working in Aruba for Lago Oil & Transport Co. There he attended Navigation School where he obtained his license as mate. He was later Captain of the 'Esso San Nicolas', 'Esso Oranjestad' and the government-owned tugboat the 'Arikok'.

On May 26th, 1959 he was elected as a member of the Island Council of Aruba. He was re-elected April 29th, 1963, and again on May 26th, 1967. In 1966, he was elected as a member of Parliament of the Netherlands Antilles. In 1969 he was re-elected and obtained the largest amount of preferential votes in the island of Aruba. He was Minister of Communication and Transportation from 1969 to 1973. He was re-elected to the Legislature in 1973, and again in 1977. Mr. Chance has been Minister of Justice and Vice Prime Minister of the Netherlands Antilles since 1976. He served almost continuously as Minister in various Cabinets from 1969 until 1987. In 1988 he was awarded the high honorary distinction of Commander of the Dutch Lion by Her Majesty Queen Beatrix of the Netherlands.

Saba's pier, a longtime dream and one of the most important contributions to the island, was the fulfillment of a dream for centuries. He was responsible for securing the funds to construct it. The WIPM government of Saba at the time decided to name the dock the Capt. Leo A.I. Chance pier, which was inaugurated on his birthday in 1972.

In September 2012 he celebrated his 80th birthday.

Tarold Hassell

Edgard Norman Tarold Hassell navegated steamships. He was the first of eight children born to Henry and Victoria Adelaide Hassell on December 22, 1892. His first wife was Estelle Praxedes Wathey from St. Maarten. After her death, he married Olive Bronte Hassell a daughter of William James Hassell Jr. and Ann Elizabeth Johnson, from Saba.

Captain of the '*Maltram*' of the 'C.D. Mallory Line', also mate on the 'Bull Line'. During World War II he was Lt. Commander in the Coast Guard around New York. Was also Chief Mate on '*Western Ocean*' a passenger ship and also rum-runner between the Caribbean and New York. Irvin Holm was Second Mate and Ainslee Peterson sailor on that same ship.

Capt. Edgar Norman Tarold Hassell

Peter John Hassell Dowling

He was a seaman born on Feb 1st, 1864, the oldest son of John Every Dowling (1836-1919) and Ann Catherine Hassell (1837-1910). His siblings were John William, George Benjamin, Ann Catherine, Judith Clara Isabel 'Sota', Alice and Ann Elizabeth Dowling.

On February 18th 1892 he married Johanna Lovelace Hassell, a daughter of Peter John 'Peniston' Hassell and Ann Catherine Hassell, and they had four children: the twins Joanna & Elizabeth, James Hallas & John Thomas Dowling.

He was Naturalized on Nov 3rd 1904 at the District Court Southern District of NY.

He died January 10th 1917 at Gulfport, Mississippi.

Ainslee Peterson

Born on May 5th 1907 he was the third child of Allen Hassell Peterson (1877-1946) and Essie Hassell (1886-1975). He married Cecile Holm, a daughter of Phoenix Lawrence Holm (1875-1957) and Mary Catherine Hassell (1883-1952), on august 28th 1928 and had seven children: Althea Elouise, Dika Bernadette, Therese, Elsa Marie, David Raymond, Agatha Phiolomena and Brenda Alice Peterson.

He developed his marine time skills with his brother Athelstan 'Attie' Peterson; we can track both of them to working of steamers such as the SS Parima, Swiftlight, Flora, Carna just to name a few.

Athelstan 'Attie' Peterson

He was the fourth child of Allen Hassell Peterson (1877-1946) and Essie Hassell (1886-1975), born on February 22nd 1909. He married Lila Blythe Hassell from Providence, RI; a daughter of Johannas Hassell from Saba and Letitia Barnett from Ireland, and had three children Gail, Cheryl and Holly Peterson.

Capt. Athelstan Peterson, his wife Lila and daughters Gail and Cheryl.

Throughout the years, there are aromas that somehow are fixated in our minds. I clearly can remember my mother's distinct smell over the years, especially on Sundays when she used her favorite perfume for church. Or my father's aftershave or hair lotion, every morning before heading out to work. Or digging in the barn at my maternal grandmother's country-style home, where she had a set of very old mahogany trunks with antique family possessions. All of these smells were brought back to my mind as I had the opportunity to review Capt. Peterson's memorabilia. I can't find words to describe my emotions as I went through the material his grandson Scott Thompson had sent. How can one describe the smell of his Continuous Discharge Book? Aromas between naphthalene balls, cedar wood and hints of a sailors cologne. Is it the sea breeze I smell? Can't quite put it in words! The "Continuous Discharge Book" was issued to a Merchant Marine and served as a certificate of identification, as well as a certificate of qualifications or service, specifying each rating in which the holder was qualified to serve on board vessels. This document was a prerequisite to employment on certain vessels of the United States. It also provides a clear record of on which ships the Merchant Marine worked and the type of voyage, either foreign or coastal.

Whether back home on Saba, or far away in USA, life was never easy for any of our seaman's wives or mothers. Especially in war times, the arrival of any letter or telegram was received with utmost expectation of happiness and at the same time dreadful fears of unwanted notices. In an era where mail was the main means of communication, one can find in these documents how feelings were poured out on those ivory pages from far away, and which could take several weeks before it reached its destiny. While at training camp, soldiers had limited time to read and write their mail, so it was not surprising that their one-page communications were rather parsimonious which left mothers and other family members upset and with thirst for more information and details. On the other hand, as they moved in the war front, letters could take a while to reach their destination. And although their sons would try to make jokes of it, they always showed their concerns for the well-being of the family.

The worst moment in the life of a war mother, wife or relative would have to be the dreaded arrival of a Western Union telegram from the War Department indicating that their soldier was missing in action or dead in some remote war-front.

Such telegram would usually be preceded by returned mail with an ink stamp which read *"Return to Sender. Addressee Reported Missing."* I can only imagine such a terrible moment when the family member would fall to their knees like a tall redwood timber chopped from below after receiving and reading such notice. Addy's wife, Lila Blythe Peterson (nee Hassell), suffered such fate when she received a telegram declaring her brother John Merwyn Hassell MIA on or about September 13th 1943. The official report was finally received almost three years later, indicating "the tug

Armitage (where he was on commission) was lost with all hands aboard between Balboa, Canal Zone (Panama) and the Galapagos Island."

War and its horrors are usually "watered down" in the history books so it was fairly difficult for people who participated in them to fence their children's questions regarding World War II. As his daughters grew up and learned more about the facts and world-politics building up to the events, as they studied Contemporary History at high school, they would ask him to share his memories of the War. Even many years after, he simply disregarded the questions saying he simply could (would) not talk about that, with clear evidence of moments he would rather like to forget.

As many of our seamen, their large merchant ships were transformed into troop carriers and supply convoys, fitted with proper defense artillery manned by the US Coast Guard, and were commanded to go into active war zones in the Pacific Ocean infested with German U-Boats. If you go to the NARA archives, you could probably trace each active soldier's whereabouts, but also diaries and family records such as Gail's Baby Book kept by his wife revealed Capt. Peterson was in the Pacific in 1944 and the "Far East" in 1945. We can only guess the deep remorse of the horrors lived; as soon as war was declared over he sold off his uniform parts at different ports on his way back home. He only kept the crest from his Officer's hat, and some metal buttons from his jacket, which his wife Lila had made into jewelry cufflinks.

Captain 'Addy' Peterson developed his marine time skills with his brother Ainslee Peterson. From his log book we can follow his progression in training from AB, LB, Second Mate, Chief Mate and until he reached his license of Master where he was at the helm of several steamships. He worked on the M/T Louraine, which provided services between New York and Caribbean ports, SS Swiftlight to Colombia and Venezuela, the SS Malabar to Curacao and other West Indies ports, SS Monocracy to England and European ports. He also worked on the SS Adrmore, SS Muskogee, and the SS Swiftsure. His last commissions as Master were aboard the SS Carbide Texas City and the SS Carbide Seadrift, based out of Texas port.

As a child, there are moments somehow fixated in our brains by some special synapsis process which makes its indelible in our minds regardless of the nature. His daughter Gail remembered vividly when her Dad was on his "runs" to Texas. She would await his return with great anticipation for gifts, of which a special one was always on her mind: a big jar of "Texas Figs!" which her mother Lila would serve with chilled fresh whipped heavy cream. In one occasion during the Christmas season, "Santa" brought Gail and Cheryl some authentic cowgirl boots. Being on a rush to get home, he probably did not notice that the pair intended for the young Cheryl actually was "high heels," so she was not able to wear hers. To Capt. Peterson's defense, "it was Santa and his dwarfs who made the mistake, not him!"

When their father was back, 'Momma Lila' always planned outings to make the most out of the time the Captain was home. They would make a "trip" to New York City; spend the afternoon skating on ice at the Rockefeller Center and end with a show at the Radio City music hall.

When the time and tides were appropriate, they could also visit Capt. Addy's ships as they pulled into New York port for maintenance or cargo load. His girls were able to board his ships and show off their natural pride; this tall and handsome man who was being saluted and "yes sired" right to left was the ship's Captain, but most importantly their father. They knew their way around and would breeze their way through the ship's hallways. As they bumped into other officers, they were given all kinds of treats, from bottles of coke to snickers bars. As they grew older, the tradition of visiting the Captain aboard also passed down to the next generation. His grandson Scott would walk up the gang plank with his "Pop Pop" as proud as peacock. The Captain as well was so proud and happy to be a grandfather. His granddaughter Nancy, took her very first wobbly steps to her "Pop Pop" aboard one of his ships, an experience which he was denied with his own children because he was on duty far away at sea.

Fortunately for Addy and his family, he was not in port when the Texas City disaster of April 16, 1947 became the deadliest industrial accident in US history, and one of the largest non-nuclear explosions, resulting from the fire on board the French-registered vessel SS Grandcamp, when its cargo of approximately 2,300 tons of ammonium nitrate exploded. This chemical compound is a crystalline powder used for military purposes mixed with TNT as a bursting charge or mixed into fertilizers as an excellent source of nitrogen for all crops. The initial blast triggered a chain-reaction of fires and explosions in other ships and nearby oil-storage facilities killing at least 581 people; the blast leveled thousands of buildings on land, destroyed the Monsanto Chemical and Union Carbide Company plants and resulted in the ignition of oil and chemical tanks on the waterfront. To understand the brute force of this explosion, in Galveston ten miles away people were forced to their knees; windows were shattered in Houston, Texas, 40 miles (60 km) away. People felt the shockwave 100 miles away in Louisiana.

Capt. Athelstan Peterson lived on, until he died on November 1978 in New Jersey, USA.

Ralph Hassell

He was born on Jan 17th 1894 to his parents John Benjamin 'Old Claw' Hassell (1849-1931) and Henrietta Johnson (1852-1914). He was the 9th child in a family of ten; his siblings were: Rupert, John Benjamin, Henry Johnson, William James Johnson, Florence, Morris, Ivan, Lily and Flossy.

He enlisted as a Seaman in WW I. He was married on September 21st 1915 to Joanna Viva Dowling, a daughter of Peter John Hassell Dowling (1864-1917) and Joanna Lovelace Hassell (1870-1946), and they had seven children: Elmer, Ivan, Muriel, Louise, Walter, John Benjamin and Velma.

He died on Saba on February 3rd 1986.

Antonio Duran Woods

Antonio was the son of Moses Woods (1874-1940) and Exerina Constantia Gordon (1874-1950). He was born December 13th 1916 and had eight siblings: Chester Hellman, Moses Clayton, Eldeca Clemencia, Martha Virginia, Uranie Leancene, Peral Pauline, Eugenia Elizabeth and Urabia Lucile Woods.

He worked for Lago Shipping Co. as a Quartermaster aboard the oil tanker SS Punta Gorda.

Died on September 18th 1944 when his ship collided with Belgian tanker SS Ampetco II; the ship caught fire and sank about 5 miles off Cabo San Roman, Venezuela (Falcon, Venezuela). On the same ship was traveling his first cousin Henry S. Woods who also died in the incident.

Richard Ludwig 'Luddie' Peterson

He was a son of Capt. John James Peterson (1862-1923) and his wife Ann Adelia Geraldine Hassell (1868-1923). He was born on December 9th 1893 and had two siblings: Vera Albertina Peterson and James Leslie Peterson.

Capt. 'Luddie' Peterson was lost a sea 1918 aboard the schooner "Arbitrator," and left no family.

Peter James Hassell

He was born on Saba on July 23rd 1881, the son of Henry Johnson Hassell (1844-1921) and Johanna Beaks (1847-1883), whose former dwelling house was the main building of the late Captain's Quarters Hotel, before its destruction beyond repairs by a hurricane. His siblings were: Ann Mary, Amy, Mabel, Henry Johnson 'Mr Heck', Ida and John Likens Hassell. His wife Emily was from Venezuela and he was the father of Norma, Peter, Emily, Gerald and George Hassell.

He was naturalized on Jun 11th 1904 at the District Court of Rhode Island. He died in New York at the age of 96, September 1977.

Augustine Johnson

He came from a large family of nine, and was the first son of Henry Hassell Johnson (1835-1920) and his wife Ann Rebecca Hassell (1842-1917). His siblings were: Moses, John Lawrence 'Toma', Caroline, Joseph Kock 'Gabo', Ina Maria, Peter, Elenor Markoe and Euphemia Johnson. He married Clara Hassell, a daughter of John Hassell (1831-1896) and Ann Catherine Hassell (1839-1928) and they had two sons: Austin and John Harold Johnson.

He was part owner and Captain of four-masted schooner named 'Robert L. Bean' and the 'Charles G. Endicott'. He used to transport coal and lumber from New York to Cadiz, Spain, and then return with olive oil and wine. His crew was from Saba.

The 'Charles G. Endicott' was about 300 feet long. Captain Irvin Holm in 1911 was a sailor on board. Other crewmembers were Wilson Johnson, cook, Thomas Charles Vanterpool, Henry Johnson, George 'Wussa' Hassell, Tom Darcy as sailors and Bloomfield Hassell as engineer. At that time, they were handling railroad ties from Savannah to New York.

Wilson Johnson, the cook, in his later years talked about the schooner. In his whole life he had seen but one schooner worth pumping out, the 'Charles G. Endicott' and but one skipper so close to God that the oats of the ship's cook fell short of the mark. He was a Saban named Augustine Johnson. "Man above men," said Wilson: a young god at sea, more n' six feet, black eyes, black mustache. Seven good years I sailed on the Endicott with'im. Let a gale come, and he'd neither eat nor drink. Stayed on the deck all the time walkin' 'round munchin'! Watchin' the sky, watchin' the riggin'! Watchin' the men. Tidin' fore the wind in a big mouthy sea. I flops on me face in the galley. Then I crawls out to see what's up. The deck she is ankle-deep in water, I feels' sum'thin' bunpin' me foot. Looking down I sees the skippers head a washing 'round like he is a dead-un. I grab 'im by the collar, pulls him outta the wet sea. A block she'd broken loose above, grazed his head, knocked two spokes outta the wheel, didn't hurt the men at the wheel, but the skipper's head was a sight. He open his eyes, gives me a long look and stumbles outside. Never says, how you be, where've I been or nuthin'! A few deep breaths, and pretty soon, he's walking 'round, munchin' air, watchin'.

He died aged 97 in Rhode Island about 1961.

John James Peterson

Capt. John James Peterson (1862-1923) married Ann Adelia Geraldine Hassell (1868-1923) on February 17, 1890, and they were the parents of Vera Albertina, Richard Ludwig 'Luddie' and James Leslie Peterson.

Captain of the three-masted schooner "James Slater" built and owned by John R. Mather of Long Island.

Capt. John James Peterson, his wife Ann Adelia Hassell and first born Vera.

Engle Heyliger Simmons

Engle Heyliger Simmons (1854-1920) was a son of John Michael Dinzey Simmons (1826-1899) and Eliza Leverock (1825-1892). In 1880 he mastered the Saban schooner 'Camelia' of 46 tons. (Notary Public in the Island of Saba in 1916.)

Emilie Elizabeth 'Berdie' Lambert (1859-1920) from Philadelphia was his wife; they were married on Saba on February 28th 1881 and were the parents of well-known Captains Evan Lambert Simmons, Engle Leverock Simmons and James Eric Simmons. Their daughters were Emelie, Elaine & Ethel Simmons.

He was politically active on the administration of the island, becoming Island Secretary and in several opportunities he served as Notary Public.

He died on September 15th 1920 at his home in The Bottom.

Edwin Rupert Simmons

Capt. Edwin Rupert Simmons

Captain Edwin Rupert Simmons (1894-1943) was the youngest son of Moses Leverock 'Pa Modie' Simmons (1848-1942) and Clementina 'Miss Clemmie' Simmons (1854-1932). He was born in Saba on August 7 1994, died and buried on St. Thomas, V.I. Was married on July 14th 1926 to Ina Vanterpool, daughter of Capt. Tommy Vanterpool, and had two children.

Before becoming a Harbour Pilot in the 1920's at Charlotte Amalie, St. Thomas, V.I., he sailed on many steamships.

During World War II he served for 22 months in the Naval Reserve Force as a Lieutenant on the USS F. J. Luckenback. This ship made her maiden voyage on January 15th 1918. She carried horses, mules and other military cargo from the U.S. to France with trips to Marseilles, St. Nazaire, Brest, and other ports during World War I. After the Armistice, she was re-fitted to carry troops back to the U.S., and with a crew of 180, she brought back 3,000 men and 75 officers.

Edwin Knight Simmons

Capt. Edwin Knight Simmons ran across the Caribbean Sea and up the Orinoco River when Standard Oil was starting to explore the expansion of the search for oil in the western the area in Venezuela.

He was a son of Joseph Dinzey Horton Simmons (1839-1905) and Margaret Jane Simmons Dinzey (1840-1897), born on Saba on July 18th 1872. His parents had a total of seven children, of which four were captains. He was a brother of Joseph Benjamin 'Blackhead Joe' Simmons, Lorenzo Simmons and Athur Wallace Simmons. His sisters were Ann Louise, Louise 'Lou' and Florence Simmons.

He married to Florence Constantia 'Florrie' Heyliger, a daughter of John Josephe Dinzey Heyliger (1829-1912) and Mary Ann 'Sis' Simmons (1834-1926), on Feb 17th 1897 and had five children: Kenneth, Lottie Constantia, Ethel Carmen, John Stanley 'Buster' and Edwin Kenneth 'Eddie' Simmons.

Capt. Knight Simmons would run up and down Demerara, and the Orinoco river with his speedy two-masted schooner *"The Cheetha,"* helping former prisoners escape, who would pay in small gold ingots to be transported to safe grounds. Once, his ship was boarded by the authorities. He ran downstairs and dropped the gold in a soup pot they were cooking and came up to walk the officers through the inspection. The authorities did not find the gold, but the Capt. was kind enough to offer a bowl of soup!

By 1929, Venezuela was the second largest oil producing country (behind only the United States) and the largest oil exporter in the world. With such a dramatic development of the industry, the oil sector had begun to dominate all other economic sectors in the country. However, most of the exploration and perforation was being done only in the western part of the country around Maracaibo Lake.

By 1938 the oil companies decided it was time to further extend their exploration operations to the east of Venezuela and as if by magic, out of nowhere, oil fields started popping-up north of Monagas: Quiriquire, Caripito and Jusepín.

Capt. Edwin Knight Simmons (third on the left) aboard The Cheetah,
entertaining some authorities off the coast of Venezuela

The lack of infrastructure forced these companies to use the rivers and streams to transport upstream everything essential to these remote places, from the most complicated rigs and equipment, to the lettuce, nuts and apples that their employees ate. From the Atlantic, down the channels of Uracoa and Manámo in the Delta and rivers Caripe, Guarapiche and San Juan navigated the 'Stanocoven' barges, Standard Oil Company of Venezuela, the predecessor of the Creole Petroleum (ESSO) Corporation.

These rivers and waters were territory all too well known by several Saban captains whom had navigated the Demerera run, helping slaves escape from Guyana and being paid in gold nuggets. Captain Knight Simmons was one of these men and in several occasions he had brought his son Stanley to learn how to navigate the murky waters of the Orinoco. His father's maps and knowledge of the area would serve him well in years to come.

As many Saban sailors, he retired to Barbados with his wife Florrie where he was always happy to receive visits from his children in company of the grandchildren; He died in May 1952.

Edwin Joseph Hill

Edwin J. Hill's birth record indicates that he was born October 4, 1894 in Philadelphia, Pennsylvania; however, according to Saban Lore his family was of Saban descent. There were two daughters of Capt. Benjamin Richard Wright Horton who married to two Hill brothers of Sint Eustatius, sons of John Heyliger Hill and Maria del Monte Martins de Clarencieux.

The Hills were a prominent white family. At that time Statia had quit a number of local white families. One of these Horton women could have been his mother and it is possible that he was born in Philadelphia. Some people even say he was born on Saba or Statia and following the tradition of many in his seafaring extended family, he may have forged an American birth certificate so that he could serve in the United States Navy. Nevertheless, I have not been able to find as of this writing any evidence in Saba's vital records that would support that as a fact. I would tend to believe his parents or grandparents were from Saba and Sint Eustatius who immigrated to the USA.

The Hill's from Saba / Statia had a rich history of seafaring, so it was the natural choice of profession for him. His uncle, Lieutenant Commander Waldron Eugene Richard David Peter Simmons, is said to have forged his own birth certificate listing Philadelphia as his "hometown" in order to enter into the U.S. Navy where he eventually served 47 years and founded the Navy base at Little Creek, Virginia.

Chief Boatswain Edwin J. Hill

Another uncle, Thomas Kane, was serving on the USS Maine as a blacksmith when it was blown up in Havana Harbor in February 1898, killing him. This bombing and destruction of the USS Maine, triggered the United States into the Spanish-American War.

He was also a cousin of Lt. Commander (and later Rear Admiral) Herman Kossler, a recipient of the Navy Cross, two Legions of Merit, and three Silver Stars; Kossler commanded the submarine USS Cavalla and radioed the position of the Japanese Fleet prior to the pivotal Battle of The Philippine Sea in 1944 (also known as "The Great Marianas Turkey Shoot").

Regardless of the question of the place of his birth, Hill enlisted in the United States Navy in 1912, and rose to the rank of Chief Boatswain. His final actions in the theater of Pearl Harbor would make for a great movie by itself.

One lazy Sunday December 7th 1941 about 7:48am local time, the United States Navy Pacific Fleet stationed in Pearl Harbor, Hawaii was surprised by a massive military attack conducted by the Imperial Japanese Navy which included the use of 353 Japanese planes including Zero fighters, Nakajima bombers, Aichi dive bombers and torpedo aircrafts in two waves launched from six aircraft carriers, as well as the use of midget submarines and other vessels. Men aboard the ships awoke to the sounds of alarms, exploding bombs, and gunfire, prompting half-awake men to dress as they ran to their assigned 'General Quarters' stations.

Last in the line-up at "Battleship Row" was a massive vessel with the designation BB-36 – the "USS Nevada." As the wave of Zeroes streaked across the Hawaii skies, a torpedo plane zoomed overhead unexpectedly, releasing a powerful bomb that scored a direct hit on the massive battleship's hull, damaging the side of the Nevada. Crews rushed to seal off decks and keep the ship from taking on water.

The Nevada's only commanding officer aboard that fatal Sunday, Ensign Joe Taussig, Jr., decided he wasn't going to be a sitting duck in what was turning out to be a Japanese target practice. As he was shouting out his orders intermixed with eloquent expletives, he realized the ship was tied down to the docks with several heavy ropes. It was then that Chief Boatswain Edwin J. Hill, sprang into action. He took a crew of sailors, sprinted from the bridge down to the pier and freed the ship, unhooking the lines and watched the Nevada slowly begin to pull away from the docks on a mad dash to get into position to fight back. Hill sprinted across the dock, while all around him things were exploding, people screaming, and Zeroes strafing the ground with machine guns. He dived into the waters of Pearl Harbor, and swam like crazy giving chase to the USS Nevada. He reached the ship, pulled himself on board, and got right back to manning his post.

As the Nevada cleared her berth and charged towards the open sea, the second wave of Japanese bombers aligned themselves for attack. By then, Hill had organized the men at their battle stations; some anti-aircraft guns made their mark, but there were simply too many bombers, and again the ship was hit with several bombs and torpedoes.

It was the wave of Aichi Dive Bombers that finally put the Nevada on the defensive. Her commander decided the only way to not suffer the same deep-death fate of the other ships was to beach the vessel in lower waters. He ordered the ship to get as close as it could to the shore and attempt to drop anchor.

Once again Edwin J. Hill was there promptly at his station. He had been managing the countless issues on the deck, making sure his crew was focused despite all the carnage and destruction going on around them. He helped the ship get into position, and personally dropping the anchor in a way that would be most advantageous for the ship to not sink to the bottom of Pearl Harbor nor block the pathway. The planes blasted the forecastle and the rear tripod mast, killing hundreds of sailors, and ignited fires in the gun casemate. As the anchor deployed he died from a close-by explosion.

Edwin J. Hill's actions on this day went beyond being an inspiration to demoralized men and women stationed at the doomed naval base. His action gave the USS Nevada a new chance to be one of three Battleships stationed at Pearl Harbor that lived to fight other important battles. From taking revenge in the attack on Okinawa, this powerful vessel also had the distinction of being the first Allied warship to fire on the coastline during the D-Day operation.

He was posthumously awarded the Navy Medal of Honor from which we read his this citation:

> *For distinguished conduct in the line of his profession, extraordinary courage, and disregard of his own safety during the attack on the Fleet in Pearl Harbor, by Japanese forces on December 7, 1941. During the height of the strafing and bombing, Chief Boatswain Hill led his men of the line handling details of the U.S.S. Nevada to the quays, cast off the lines and swam back to his ship. Later, while on the forecastle, attempting to let go the anchors, he was blown overboard and killed by the explosion of several bombs.*

The Edsall-class destroyer escort DE-141, was named USS Hill in honor of Chief Boatswain Edwin J. Hill, who lost his life in his brave actions during the attack on Pearl Harbor.

Waldron Eugene Richard David Peter Simmons

Captain Waldron Eugene Richard David Peter Simmons, was born on February 3rd 1879. His place of birth has not yet been properly established. Apart from Will Johnson's information in his book "Saban Lore: Tales from my Grandmother's Pipe" I have not found information regarding his birth record in Saba's Vital Records. We have to rely on Waldron's own declarations to the US Censuses (1910, 1920, 1930 & 1940) where he declares as born in Brooklyn, New York.

He was a son of Peter Simmons (1858-1894) and Inez Dinzey Horton (1853-1879), both from Saba, and had two siblings: Edward Clinton and Ethel Simmons.

He left Saba with his father, Captain Peter Simmons on long trips at the early age of twelve and worked in different capacities learning the trade directly from his father. He sailed with him to San Francisco via Cape Horn, and a while later they visited Australia. His love for the sea was established at this earlier date, as his respect and ties to his father also grew. He remained in New York studying while his father returned to Saba, however he was lost in a storm off Cape Hatteras on the way down.

Captain Waldron Eugene Richard David Peter Simmons

Waldron's naval career officially began January 23rd 1895, at a ripe age of seventeen but with already many years of hardened experience from his young sailing days with his father. He was awarded the Gold Life-Saving Medal and the Baily Medal, the latter going to the apprentice seaman having the highest grade upon 'graduation' from boot-camp. This allowed him to promptly take part in the Spanish-American War fought in Cuba. He saw action from aboard the "USS Massachusetts." He was also in China for the Boxer Rebellion and served in both World Wars.

He climbed the ladder with perseverance and hard work, and by 1909 he was appointed Warrant Boatswain. He reached the rank of Chief Boatswain and placed on retirement after seven years, which would only last for only two months as he was recalled to active duty in September 1916 in light the declaration of World War I. His assignment at that time was the receiving ship and training station at St. Helena, Va., where he served as Assistant XO.

He married Blanche Marie Barraud, a daughter of Eugene Armand Barraud from Bordeaux, France and Mary Ann Kane from Dublin, Ireland on September 30th 1908. Their marriage was blessed with five children: Inez Mathilde 'Nezzie', Katherine 'Kitty', Waldron Peter Jr., Blanche 'Bumpy' and Octavia Anne 'Honey' Simmons. At the end of WW I, he went to work in the Norfolk Navy Yard where he made Portsmouth, Virginia his home.

He had a brother named Clinton who married a lady, Nellie DeGraff, from St. Thomas. Their son, George Renald Simmons served as Administrator of St. John in the U.S. Virgin Islands for nearly ten years.

Again he retired, only to be called back to take part in in World War II being assigned to the naval Frontier Base at Little Creek. He remained in active duty, and rose to the rank of Lieutenant Commander.

He died at the age of 69 in the Portsmouth, VA on September 22nd 1948.

Harold Christopher Simmons

He was born on December 26th 1884 on Saba, the second son of Samuel Augustus 'Sam' Simmons Sr. (1848-1930) and Eva Johnson (1863-1946), and had eight siblings: Samuel Augustus Jr., Solomon (who fell off a tree trying to catch a bird and died young), Ivy Clayton, Cameron Dudley, Essie Florence, Pansy Camelia 'Nanny', Solomon Ashley and John Simmons. He married Isabelle "Belle" Williams from Louisiana and has two children, Harold and Audrey.

He immigrated to the USA in 1896 according to the 1910 US Census, and was already naturalized by the time of the enumeration (May 10, 1910)

Harold (23) & his brother Samuel Augustus (26) were aboard the SS *Trinidad* as seamen (both listed as single), Sailing from Bermuda March 9, 1907 Arrived at the Port of New York, March 1907. They are identified as US Citizens.

Harold Christopher Simmons, Captain (license 797) of SS *"The Mielero"* arrived with his family at New York, NY on July 30, 1919 from the port of Antilla, Cuba; he was 5-8 in height and weight 175lbs. This ship had several other Saban hands: Rufus Constantine Blyden (Boatswain), Simon Hughes, Alexander Simmons, Epolite Hassell, William Wilson, Octavus Oswald Hassell (all AB Sailors).

In March 4, 1914 he was commanding the SS "Charlemagne Tower Jr.," a bulk wooden-freighter built in 1886 at Cleveland, Ohio by the Thomas Quale and Son shipyard, and owned by the Southern Steamship Co. The ship was sailing from Norfolk to Boston with a full load of coal. Although the ship had been out of commission for six years it was considered seaworthy. About six miles out, a bad snow storm and faulty motor made Capt. Simmons turn the ship back, but the seams busted open and started to sink rapidly. The water poured in at such a rate, that two hours later the ship was filled to her upper beams. Immediately they set up the distress signals and sent out wireless calls which were picked up by the Sandy Hook Station as well as the Old Dominion liner SS "Hamilton". Incredibly the Hamilton after establishing and confirming via wireless the position of the distressed freighter, they continued their planned route to

New York. The crew of the "Charlemagne Tower Jr." hardly had time to get into the two small boats before the ship plunged to her final fate.

Capt. Simmons later declared that the Hamilton passed near his ship when they were barely afloat, and his ship was displaying at the time the signal *"We are sinking: send lifeboats"*. He said the Hamilton answered, but made no attempt to rescue the ship, not even stop to investigate! "I am making no direct charge against the captain of the Hamilton" said Capt. Simmons, "but if I were a Captain of a passing steamer and saw such signal displayed, with a crowd of men huddled in a lifeboat near the sinking vessel, I should have investigated." He added, "I know that the Hamilton saw the signal for she replied, 'I don't understand, will report,' and went on."

The escape of the survivors was a narrow one. One small lifeboat with four crew members was able to pass the breakers and make it to shore, but the captain was not willing to risk the 18 men aboard the larger lifeboat so aimed his boat out to sea. They hoisted a light which was barely visible through the blinding snow-storm and the gripping darkness of night. Off Barnegat, NJ they were sighted by Capt. Beranger of the whaleback ship 'Bayport' just as she was passing by the boat. Some of the Saba men sailing with Capt. Simmons on this trip were Quartermaster John Dowling and Messman Ralph Holm[6]. The Captain and the rest of the crew were given food and accommodations and delivered to port safely.

As WW I in Europe was raging, America was not yet involved. A large schooner was sailing on a cold winter day, crossing somewhere in the middle of the Atlantic Ocean. Suddenly a German U-boat broke from beneath the waves near the bow of the ship -- the crew called their Captain. Shots were fired in the air and German sailors with blazing guns boarded the deck of the ship. As the German Captain boarded, he ordered the enemy crew to search the ship. The Schooner's Captain and

---

[6] Some people from Saba adopted the surname *'Holmes'* as they completed immigration process to USA and also Bermuda.

German Captain talk. From below the main-deck a woman's voice (with a New Orleans accent) was heard:

"Who are you? What right do you have on my husband's ship?"

The woman was lead up the stairs to the main-deck, escorted by armed German sailors. She carried her two children, a little boy and a baby girl. The woman marched up to the enemy Captain and again demanded, "Who are you? What right do you have on my husband's ship?"

The German captain looked at her and in broken English began to address her. But the woman refused to hear the intruder. She told him, "As long as there are Stars and Bars, and as long as my husband is Captain of this ship, you are not welcomed on board!" told

With her words, the German Captain turned to the Schooner's Captain, made an 'impolite' comment about the woman. He then called the boarding crew and left the schooner without taking anything or injuring anyone. In those days, it was customary that U-boats would raid passing merchant ships for supplies. The woman, and her headstrong personality, was credited for chasing the enemy captain away. Family lore says something about the German Captain telling the Captain that he had enough to deal with concerning the woman, and kind of felt sorry for him having the woman aboard.

The Captain was Harold Christopher Simmons; the woman was his wife, Belle, and their two children Harold Jr. and daughter Audrey.

A typical entry in the manifests for the ship would be:

SS Mielero *"Manifest of Aliens Employed on the Vessel as Member of the Crew"* is his family: (Lines 40-42)

> 40. SIMMONS, Mrs. H. C – *Stewardess* (B63730), age 30, height 5'4" and Weight 150lbs
> 41. SIMMONS, Harold C. Jr. – *Cabin Boy*
> 42. SIMMONS, A.F – *Girl*

In 1920, their ship went to Galveston for repairs. After the repairs were made, the ship was moored in nearby docks to take on goods. A storm happened, and the ship hit the side of the pier. Although a routine inspection was done, no one found any damage to the hull.

The ship went out to sea with its cargo, traveling through the Caribbean and South Atlantic. The ship encountered another storm. The damaged hull cracked and the ship broke in two.

The crew made it on one lifeboat including his brother-in-law Allen Holbrook who was the ship's Chief Engineer; Harold, Belle, their children and other crewmembers, on another. The lifeboats were kept together with a rope, and adrift on the open sea. After three days without food and water, things were really bad. Harold's daughter Audrey was dying and their lifeboat was taking on water. It was decided to remove the rope, and let the lifeboats separate. Waves drifted the lifeboats apart until a big wave came and separated the two boats from view. The SS Mielero went down in January 26th 1920 around 0700, about 100 miles SE of Osaba Island in Georgia.

It was only three or four hours after the separation decision was made that a passing steamer, "the Ozette", found one of the lifeboats - it was the one with the crew. They searched for three days, but never found the other lifeboat with Harold, his family and other crew members.

At the Coast Guard Inquiry regarding this incident, it was determined that the hull must have been damaged on the pier during the storm at Galveston. Also, it is interesting to note that Harold Simmons Jr. was listed as crew aboard the ship although he was only about 8 years old. It was decided at this inquiry that the U.S. would never again allow a crewmember of a ship to be so young.

Harold Christopher Simmons did not always include the name "Christopher." Back in the day, when he went to get his Master's license, he added the second name "Christopher," on the fly. He saw that most of the American merchant captains used two names, so he "adopted" the middle name Christopher (patron saint of sailors, who protects travelers against turbulent waters).

The tank-ship Mielero, the third of its design, built by the Fore River Shipbuilding Co., was launched January 23rd, from the Fore River Ship yards[7]. It was built for the Cuba Distilling Company of New York and designed primarily for the carrying of molasses in bulk, but it was so arranged that she may also be employed in the carriage of bulk petroleum. Her configuration as a carrier was unique in that while she carried molasses in bulk in her trips north from Cuba she would return south with petroleum in bulk without the need of renovating her tanks at either end of the voyage.

The molasses carried is not the familiar commodity but a by-product from which the sugar has been extracted, used for distilling and other industrial purposes. The vessel had a carrying capacity of about 1,500,000 gallons of molasses and about 2,250,000 gallons of oil, the cargo dead weight being over 8,000 tons.

The liquid cargo was discharged by an elaborate system of pumps connected to a 14-inch main pipe. Special accommodations were available to the officers and crew.

The propelling machinery consisted of one vertical triple-expansion engine driving a right-hand propeller, steam being supplied from three single-ended boilers.

Peter Simmons

Peter Simmons was born on September 7th 1858 on Saba, the youngest son of Edward Simmons (1802-1872) and Margaret Toland (1809-1892); she was from Antigua. His siblings were Edward Simmons Jr. and Georgianna Ekerman (nee Simmons).

He was married on March 19th 1875 to Inez Dinzey Horton (1853-1879), the third daughter of Benjamin Richard Wright Horton (1823-1869) and Johanna Dinzey Heyliger (1827-1897). They had two children which are

---

[7] The American Marine Engineer, Volume 12, Nbr. 3, Page 7 - National Marine Engineers' Beneficial Association (U.S.) – March 1917

recorded on the Virgin Islands census records of 1880: Edward Clinton and Waldron Eugene Richard David Peter Simmons. On this same record we find evidence of a second marriage to a lady Erneste or Ernestine Simmons.

Peter Simmons was captain of the schooner (four-masted barkentine) '*William P. Frye*' built in Bath, Maine.

January 27th, 1915. Schooner '*William P. Frye*', gross 3374 tons was captured by German auxiliary cruiser Prinz Eithel Frederick in South Atlantic southeast of Brazil. Sunk on January 28th, 1915. No casualties. First United States registered vessel sunk in WW I.

He was lost off Cape Hatteras in another schooner; I think it was the "*Sprague*" in 1897.

Henry Swinton Woods

Born on January 17th 1912 to Joseph Benjamin 'Joe Ben' Woods (1877-1970) and Anna Minita Warner (1881-1935).

He was a Quartermaster aboard the oil tanker Punta Gorda, property of Lago Shipping Co. Notably he was a survivor of the attack and sinking of tanker SS San Nicolas on 16 February 1942.

He died on September 18th 1944, when his ship collided with Belgian tanker Ampetco II, near Cabo San Roman (Venezuela) on the same ship as his cousin Antonio Duran Woods.

Engle 'Engie' Leverock Simmons

Engle Leverock Simmons (1890-1972) was the middle son of Engle Heyliger Simmons and Emilia Elizabeth Lambert. His brothers were Evan Lambert Simmons and James Eric 'Jim' Simmons, who also became ship captains.

Engle Leverock Simmons

After completing the 8th grade in a one room schoolhouse on Saba, Engle went to sea at age 14 as a cabin boy. He was a natural at sea, and by age twenty he had earned his Master's License and was sailing on wooden schooners out of New York before settling in St. Thomas.

Captain William 'Will' Octavius Simmons was a boyhood friend and mentor. He got jobs for Engle and his brother Jim in Santo Domingo. Engle's first job was with the government of Santo Domingo patrolling the river on Cutter #4 and fighting off rebels.

Engle was made captain of the "Caribe," a ship owned by the sugar company. He was on the deck of the Caribe when it exploded in the harbor in 1916. He was knocked unconscious by the explosion and thrown into the water. One of the United States marines who were guarding the harbor dived into the floating debris and pulled him out of the water. Engle had burns on his head and shoulders but survived the blast. It has been speculated that the explosion was the result of a German sabotage.

The Captain and his wife Estelle Vanterpool

In 1917 Captain Will Simmons moved to St. Thomas and again got Engle a job as a pilot with the Harbormaster's office. Subsequently Engle's brother Jim Simmons and Capt. Edwin Rupert Simmons came to St. Thomas as harbor pilots. Engle and Jim both served as Harbormaster.

Many of the vessels entering the harbor of Charlotte Amalie were of foreign registry and some of the captains did not speak English. Captain Engie and Capt. Jim both had to learn navigation commands in Spanish, French, German, Russian, and several other languages to guide the ships safely into the harbor.

As Harbormaster, one of Captain Engle's duties was issuing weather alerts and hurricane warnings for the U.S. Virgin Islands. His office was responsible for telegraphing weather reports to San Juan, Puerto Rico at 8:00 A.M. and 5:00 P.M. daily and more often in hurricane season. During World War II, coded reports were sent at 2:00 A.M., 8:00 AM, 2:00 PM and 8:00 PM. After the war, the responsibility for weather reports was transferred to the FAA at St. Thomas airport. Upon retirement his pension from the Weather Bureau was actually greater than that of Harbormaster.

In addition to his position as Harbormaster, Captain Engle was the St. Thomas agent for Lloyds of London. In this capacity he inspected damaged vessels and assisted with insurance settlements

Engle and his wife Estelle (Vanterpool) raised five sons and one daughter on St. Thomas. With little formal training, he and his brothers Jim and Evan mastered the ever-changing skills of navigation, communication, weather forecasting, and administrative responsibilities. They started as cabin boys on wooden schooners and ended their careers at the helms of some of the largest cargo, passenger, and cruise ships ever built. A great testimony to the seafaring men of the little island of Saba.

James Eric 'Jim' Simmons

Capt. Jim Simmons (left) with his Brother-in-law Commodore Thomas Simmons and his wife Ottlie Simmons

Capt. Jim was born on Saba on August 9th 1892. He came from a family of other famous sea captains. He was son of Engle Heyliger Simmons (1854-1920) and his wife Emilie Elizabeth 'Berdie' Lambert (1859-1920). Berdie's parents, Frederick & Susan Lambert, were from St. Barths, but she was born in Philadelphia, PA. His siblings were: Emilie, Elaine 'Ellie', Evan Lambert and Engle Leverock Simmons.

As many Sabans, Captain Jim after navigating many sea routes he looked for a more stable income and environment to raise his family and followed his brother and cousin to Dominican Republic. On July 1st 1914 he joined the Dominican Customs Service as a Pilot Captain.

He participated in the rescue of a shipwreck off the coast of Dominican Republic in early 1919 where he pulled out of the water a fellow named Otto Thomas Leoke, who happened to be an Estonian Merchant Marine and assistant engineer at the Dominican Republic Customs Service. Capt. Jim rescued him and another fellow from a shipwreck and brought them home for dinner. There Otto met Jim's sister-in-law, Irene there who had come from Saba to assist her sister Ottie with Lucy's birth. It was love at first sight!

Otto and Irene were married on Oct 15, 1919, lived in La Romana and had six children. Otto was a ship captain for Puerto Rico Sugar Co. He died of a heart attack as he was climbing out of his boat unto the dock on March 31, 1945.

The Leoke family remained in the DR but eventually Helen and Dorothy went to New York to live with their uncle Commodore Thomas Simmons and Aunt Enid May in Long Island; they returned to the DR but came back to the USA when Dorothy married John Stroyvus. Helen came up to be with her sister Dorothy. Irene lived the rest of her life residing a few months at a time with her daughters in the USA and her daughters in the DR, where she finally died in January 1979.

Capt. Jim continued to work as a harbor pilot in Santo Domingo for the Dominican Republic Government under the dictatorship of Rafael Trujillo (aka "El Jefe"). On the side, he would also bring in Molasses tankers for extra money.

It is not clear if Capt. Jim had a confrontation with Dictator Trujillo, or it was simple mismanagement of the Customs Services Department, but he had not been paid for over a year. He literally relied and sustained his family on the income he was making by bringing in the molasses tankers. Another possibility was that Trujillo had held his pay in retaliation because his brother, Engle, who had left Dominican Republic to follow Captain William Octavius Simmons as he became the Harbor Master in St. Thomas, USVI.

Captains Evan Lambert Simmons, William Octavius Simmons, James Eric Simmons & Engle Leverock Simmons

Capt. Jim, as many other Sabans, was a Free Mason, and a fellow Mason used his influence and government connections to get Jim all of his back pay. Upon receiving his money Jim, his wife Ottillie, daughters Ethel Charmaine, Lucy and Edna boarded a schooner (possibly owned by Otto Leoke) and escaped in the middle of the night leaving most of their possessions behind, fleeing to St. Thomas. His daughters, Mary and Stella were in NYC with Jim's sister Elaine, attending school.

Months later, Trujillo's yacht pulled into St. Thomas, and Trujillo requested to see Capt. Jim; he was fearful, but went to see Trujillo anyway. It was then that Trujillo asked Jim to pilot his private yacht. Jim declined (which was quite bold; not many people would say 'No' to a dictator), but since Trujillo's yacht was on US waters, we guess he felt a little less intimidated by Trujillo.

Another thing I had been told was that Jim had been looking for a way to get out of Dominican Republic for quite a while, because Trujillo had five sons, and Jim had five daughters. Jim and his family were always invited to parties and social events. And with all of this interaction due to his position, Jim was not about to let any of his daughters be pursued by Trujillo's sons.

He died June 26th 1977 in Jacksonville, Florida.

William Octavius 'Will' Simmons

William was the oldest son of Edmond Rudolph Simmons (1848-1916) and Ann Posie 'Tanta' Simmons (1851-1928). His siblings were: Amy, Edith, Ann and Anlire Simmons.

He followed his father's tradition and captained the 'Endymion', a two-masted vessel featuring a steel frame built to withstand "many a gale". At the age of 19 he was already the Captain and part owner of a large four-masted schooner the 'Andrew Adams' and used to sail around the world. His entire crew was from Saba, including Rupert Hassell (Chief Mate), Rudolph Simmons (Second Mate), Dory Heyliger (Engineer), Peter Hassell (Sailor) Ronald Hassell (Steward), Peter Every (Sailor) and Carl Hassell (Cabin Boy). Naturalized on May 15th 1899 at Circuit Court of Boston, Mass.

He worked as Custodian and Supply officer at the Dominicans Customs Service since May 20, 1907. He later moved to St. Thomas where he became Harbour Master.

On February 1st, 1928 an emergency meeting was held at Harmonic Lodge to confer honorary membership to Bro. Col. Charles A. Lindberg. At 11:15 a.m., Bro. Lindberg was escorted to the Lodge by Past Masters Wor. Bro. John N. Lightbourn, Wor . Bro. Dr. Knud Knud-Hansen, and

Bro. William Octavius Simmons. The Master addressed the distinguished guest, presented him with the speech and a souvenir which was a silver trowel with a gold handle, suitably inscribed. Bro. Lindberg thanked the Brethren.

Charles A. Lindbergh was a Mason. He visited St. Thomas with the "Spirit of St. Louis" when returning to the United States after his "Latin-America Goodwill" tour through Central America to Panama, then surveyed the route up the chain of islands back to Miami for Pan American. He landed at Mosquito Bay on January 31, 1928, and spent several days there. The "Spirit of St. Louis" hangs in the Smithsonian Museum in Washington. The flags of all the countries he visited are painted on the engine cowl. The U.S. Virgin Islands flag is among them. Lindbergh was made an honorary member of Harmonic Lodge (356) on February 1, 1928.

Evan Lambert Simmons

He was the son of the well-known Island Secretary Engle Heyliger Simmons and his wife Emilie Elizabeth 'Birdie' Lambert who was born in Philadelphia, USA. Born on August 28th 1888, he was brother of Emilie and Elaine Simmons, as well as other distinguished Saba Captains: Capt. Engle Leverock Simmons and Capt. James Eric 'Jim' Simmons whom we cover under separate sections.

He became a citizen on 16 July 1912; listed address was 4 Fulton St, New York City, NY.

He first married a girl from Statia, Maria Lillian Hill, daughter of Theodore Godet Heyliger Hill and Robertina Dinzey Horton, and had four children Elaine, Ethel, Evan Leslie and James Lambert. The Hill's Family of Sint Eustatius and the Horton's of Saba had several marriages together. On a trip to Statia to visit her parents, the couple lost a child not a year old yet, named Ethel who died on May 12th, 1918. The baby is listed as having been born in Brooklyn where the couple then lived.

Eric Simmons mentioned in a letter to Will Johnson that he considered his uncle Evan a real hero. He got to know him well while he was attending College on the East Coast. At that time he worked for the "Red D Line", Captain of the SS Lara. He was also Captain of a supply vessel, which took part in the D-Day invasion of Normandy during WW II. He also was captain for the Grace Lines in New York on the ships "Santa Rosa" and also the "Santa Ana".

It seems his first big commission started in 1918 being the First Officer of the SS Maracaibo. From then on, he was engaged with seafaring activities until the mid-1950's when he retired. Some of the ships he commanded were: SS Maracaibo, SS Caracas, SS Carabobo, SS Lara, SS Trujillo, SS Santa Ana, SS Santa Barbara and SS Santa Catalina.

The 'Red D Line' was one of the few American steamship companies that survived the depression. For half a century the ships of this line had been plying between New York and Puerto Rico and the ports of Maracaibo, La Guaira, and Puerto Cabello in Venezuela via Curacao. Once every week on Curacao one could expect to see one of their ships arrive in the harbor of Willemstad. They would stay a day and then proceed to La Guaira, Puerto Cabello and Maracaibo, and make another stop at Curacao on the return journey to New York.

In an article for the State Department in the nineteen thirties the American Consul said:

"The Captains of these 'Red D Line' ships became our fast friends and lunched or dined with us as regularly as their ship came into port. Food was always a difficult problem on the island as owing to the lack of rain it was impossible to raise cattle other than goats. What these latter lived on it would be very difficult to determine. They nibbled away at the cactus, pushing away the sharp spines with their forefeet, and in some way they were able to reach the succulent leaves of the few small trees that flourish in spite of the arid soil. The ordinary meat that we consumed was from lean cattle brought from Venezuela and Colombia and slaughtered on the same day on which it was consumed. In those days there were no adequate refrigerating facilities on the island to keep meat. The Captains of these "Red D Line" steamers brought with them in the ice box of the ship choice morsels of beef, lamb and veal, which were a rich addition to our larder, and they brought us many other delicacies which we would otherwise have to go without."

Evan grew up on Saba at a time when "the sea was everything" to the young men. Many in the Simmons family owned schooners or were captains so young boys back then started embracing sea as young as thirteen. Evan and his brothers were no exception.

He arrived the first time to USA in 1906 aboard the Schooner 'Herald' as a cabin-boy; in 1907 he was a passenger of 17 years old on the SS Trinidad, coming to New York probably with the intentions to stay and complete his education in preparation for Steam ships.

The Saba School of Navigation had not yet been officially recognized by the Dutch. However many of the retired captains, for a small monthly fee, were willing to give lessons to the young boys concerning navigation, ports they had been to, horror stories of going around Cape Horn and so on. So when Evan went to the United States he was well prepared for a life at sea.

Captain Evan has a number of descendants living in the United States still. On the Amazon.com website there is a comment regarding Will Johnson's book *"Tales from my Grandmother's Pipe"* dated September 12th, 2010, written by Evan's grandson who had the following to say:

"This book has a special meaning for me in that the island of Saba is the birthplace of my Grandfather, Captain Evan L. Simmons, pictured at age 13 on page 72. He was born August 28, 1888 and passed away on January 30th, 1966. My grandson, his great-great grandson, Evan Simmons the fifth, shares his same birthday. I have fond memories of him singing sea shanties to me before falling off to sleep, and his story that I am a descendant of Henry Morgan the pirate. I am fortunate to have his sextant. I will be visiting Saba for the first time next year and this book will provide a wonderful guide for the visit. Evan Simmons."

When his first wife died in 1958, Capt. Evan married Olga May Simmons, a daughter of Capt. Arthur Wallace Simmons (1875-1934) and Mildred Simmons (1879-1932). She was born in Brooklyn, NY on Nov 26th 1917 and together they had a daughter. That lifelong sea breeze had done wonders for the captain as he was seventy one at the time of his last child's birth!

He died at the age of 77, on Jan 30th 1966 in Brooklyn, NY.

Bernard 'Ben' Leverock

Ben was the fourth child born to the marriage of Jacob Hassell Leverock (1860-1930) and Esther Erlvine 'Hetty' Leverock, who had a total on nine children. His siblings were Elizabeth, Ivy, Alda, James Anthony, MacDonald, Darrell, Lila Joseline 'Lita' and Orlie Clive Leverock. He married a lady Josephine from St. Kitts, but as the date of this book I had not uncovered any children.

Ben Leverock, as many from Saba started off on sail and then progressed to steam. He last visited Saba in June 1981. As a young boy, he sailed around the West Indies on two schooners, namely the *'Nicola'* and the *'Golden West II'*. The Captains of these schooners were Sabans.

He enlisted for WW I when he was Third Officer working for Standard Oil, on June 5 1917. From his records we can tell he was a tall and thin man at 6 ft tall and 155 pounds of weight. He was living with his mother at 8632 107st, Richmond Hill, NY.

In May 23 1919 he was the Chief Officer of the SS Santa Elena arriving at the Port of New York from the port of Colon, Panama; his brother Donald was the Third Mate.

His vision of becoming a full fledge Captain was clear from early age. At age 25 he had already become a US Citizen by naturalization at Boston, Mass. and in 1924, he became Third Officer of a steam ship.

Ben worked for Luckenback Steam Ship Co. and was captain of the "Lena Luckenback." He also held a pilot's license and it is said could dock the "Lena Luckenback" at the 35 St Pier in Brooklyn NY without aid of a tugboat.

In 1940, he was promoted to Captain of the 12,000 ton steamboat 'Paul Luckenbach' and of course was Captain during World War II. When Captain of the U.S. Government owned vessel the SS "*Lynchburgh*", and as the vessel was passing through the Great Barrier Reef to the east of Australia, he sighted two life boats with men in them. He stopped his ship and rescued the survivors who were Australians; their ship had run aground. Bernard made twenty seven trips as Captain between New Guinea and Australia. He was Captain of Luckenbach ships for eighteen years and the United States Marine shops for six years. He was an officer of about 16 different ships: Chief Mate of the SS Dorothy Luckenbach, Second-Mate of the SS Harry Luckenbach and Master of the SS Walter A. Luckenbach and the SS Mary Luckenbach which serviced the Korean and Japan ports to Portland, Oregon.

On one trip, carrying cargo to communist China during the Korea War, he fell and sliced open his leg. The Chinese would not allow the crew ashore or anyone on to the boat, so Ben had to be his own surgeon and stitched up his leg. This incident made the New York Times.

Once, while in command of the SS "*Gathling*," the under section of the ships rudder fell off six hundred miles to the East of Bermuda during the last World War. The fastest ship he was ever Captain of was SS "*Mexico Victory*" (VC2-S-AP3 January 26, 1944 / March 27, 1944 / May 19, 1944). Her top speed was twenty-two knots.

Captain Leverock retired in 1964 and died in 1988 in Pinellas Co., FL.

Samuel Augustus Simmons Sr.

He was the son of John 'Coonks' Simmons and Ann Eliza Hassell, born about 1849 and also brother to Solomon 'Butchie' Simmons. He married Eva Johnson (1863-1946) from St. Michaels, Barbados but of Saban parents, John William Johnson (1825-1896) and Johanna 'Hanna' Simmons. Captain Simmons and his wife Eva had a total of nine children, however not all of them survived: Samuel Augustus Jr., Harold Christopher, Solomon (who died at young age), Ivy Clayton, Cameron Dudley, Essie Florence, Pansy Camelia 'Nanny', Solomon Ashley and John Simmons.

The sea stole Miss Eva and Captain Sammy of three sons. One of them Captain Harold C. Simmons was lost with his entire family in the Gulf of Mexico. He was captain of the SS *"Mielero,"* a molasses tanker that broke in two during a storm. They were able to get into lifeboats, one of which with a David Johnson from Saba made it safely to shore.

We have seen the report made after the disaster happened and the lifeboat carrying the Captain and his family was lost with all on board. Earlier, with Captain Ralph Holm on board as a mate, Captain Harold was shipwrecked on a coal boat that sank on route from Philadelphia to Boston. On that trip, all lives were saved.

Capt. Sammy also commanded the first of the Saba-owned mail boats entering the scene on June 21st, 1911, using his schooner "Priscilla" as evidenced from the following agreement:

1st. Albert Land, temporary Administrator of Finances as appointed by Government, and

2nd. Capt. Samuel Augustus Simmons, captain of the Dutch schooner "Priscilla" with 69 registered tons and belonging to Saba, do hereby declare to have made the following contract with regard to a voyage to the Islands St. Maarten, Sint Eustatius and Saba and return, under the following conditions:

1st. That the schooner be perfectly seaworthy properly crewed and in every respect equipped to leave on this voyage on the 23rd instant with destination to the aforementioned islands.

2nd. that the schooner must call twice at each of these islands, once to land the mails and once to take the mails.

3rd. that the government will pay to the contracting party Simmons on his arrival at Curacao, the sum of three hundred and seventy five guilders for the transport of mails and other government goods.

4th. that for government passengers of Curacao to one of the islands aforementioned shall be paid to the contracting party Simmons: for each first class passenger, with luggage the sum of forty guilders and for each second class passenger, with luggage, the sum of twenty guilders.

5th. that feeding of the government passengers, shall be at the expense of the contracting party Simmons.

He also purchased for $600, the eighty-two ton American schooner "William J. Smith" from its previous owner Mr. Henry A. Varatable from New York in a transaction where his brother Solomon Simmons sold the ship acting by virtue of a Power of Attorney. I would not be surprised that Solomon helped his brother get a good deal on the ship!

Samuel Augustus Simmons Jr.

Capt. Sammy Simmons was the first child of Samuel Augustus Simmons Sr. (1849-1930) and Eva Johnson (1863-1946), born on Saba on March 18th 1881. His siblings were: Harold, Solomon, Ivy Clayton, Cameron Dudley, Essie Florence, Pansy Camelia "Nanny", Solomon Ashley and John Simmons.

Capt. Samuel Augustus Simmons Jr.

He married first to Alaine Vanterpool (a daughter of John Pitman Vanterpool and Georgiana Simmons) on September 8th 1909; his second wife was Ruby Willis Manning and they had two surviving children: Stella Augusta Simmons and Harold 'Harry' Elton Simmons.

We can track many of his movements into the New York port as early as May 08, 1903 when he arrives aboard the SS Korona following the call of the likes of John Johnson, Richard S. Winfield and Arthur W. Simmons. He established residence in Mystic, Conn. Naturalized at Circuit Court US District of Boston, Mass on April 15th, 1904.

He was master of the SS Sucrosa, the sister ship of the SS Mielero, a 406' Tanker owned by Cuba Dist. Co. This boat was commissioned on 30 June 1916 and scrapped in 1946. Several Saban sailors were on this ship as well: Engle Heyliger, James Knight Simmons, Anthony Simmons, Albert A.

Holbrook. He would many times travel aboard the SS Vasari with his brother Cameron D. Simmons, from Barbados.

He was active seaman until 1939 when he was assigned as Harbor Captain for Marine Transport Lines.

After the death of his wife Ruby Manning, Capt. Samuel Simmons decided it would be better for him to enter the facilities of Sailors' Snug Harbor, not wanting to become a burden for his married children. From the moment he arrived there, like good sailors do, he immediately got along well with many of his confreres and made many friends amongst his mates as well as the staff.

He talked with one and all of his great deal of pride in his family and made it a point to introduce them to everyone every time they came to visit him. He was always anxious to do whatever task was assigned to him and took joy in performing them unusually well as if it was a vital task on a ship.

He enjoyed small manual tasks and got into the hobby of weaving. To that effect he built his own loom in his room and made numerous scarves, which he would give out as gifts, of even sell a few for profit. He was very pleased of the praise he received for these hand-made objects.

He also had a tendency to boast a great deal about his unusual good health for a man his age. He thought that in spite of his years he was quite capable of getting around with much more agility than a younger person. And this appeared to be true, as he would deliver many messages to the various buildings, briskly climbing several flights of steps. He would tally the steps and proudly report his total.

His good health and comfortable state continued until about March 1968 when he began to complain about dizzy spells. At one time he was standing in front of his dresser combing his hair when he turned too quickly and had a sudden sense of weakness with the movement and fell to the floor striking his head. He received a laceration to the scalp and was immediately taken to the infirmary where they stitched him up. For several days he was comfortable but his restless spirit made him feel confined there. As he left the infirmary he jokingly said he would have to exercise his "sailor legs" again because he felt overall weak.

He tried to gain his rhythm back, but his faltering health was pulling him down. Over the next several months he would be in and out of the infirmary for one reason or the other, until he was finally placed there in October 1970.

After 45 years (30 as a merchant off-shore, 15 as a coastal merchant) at sea and nine years at the Snug Harbour, he let down his sails quietly, with the final rise of the sun on December 18th 1970.

Cameron Dudley Simmons

I was fortunate to have met his youngest daughter, my cousin Edna Louise Brown, who always had a glitter of keen admiration and love in her eyes for her father Capt. Cameron Dudley Simmons. He was born on Saba and his wife was Edna Blanche Simmons born 1904, who was a daughter of Captain Solomon "Butchie" Simmons. Her mother was Eugenie Bruce, a daughter of Charles Bruce, the Customs Collector in Montego Bay; he and his wife were from Scotland.

With only 19 years of age he was already the master of the SS Bulko. Eager to not leave his young family behind, on a trip from Sagua La Grande, Cuba arriving at the port of NY, on Sept 15th 1925, his wife Edna Blanche Simmons (21) is listed as a Stewardess, same for their daughter Marjorie Thelma, and son Sydney Augustus, stewardess and messboy respectively, although they were only 2 & 4 years old.

He was a son of Captain Samuel Augustus Simmons and Eva Simmons (nee Johnson) from St. Michaels, Barbados. Captain Sammy was born on Saba and filled many functions in the Saba government administration at the time. His siblings, also raised in the seafaring business were: Samuel Augustus Jr., Harold 'Christopher', Solomon, Ivy Clayton, Essie Florence, Pansy Camellia, Solomon Ashley and John.

His mother, "Miss Eva" was descended from a branch of the Johnson family who moved back and forth between Saba and Barbados. Although she was born on Barbados, her parents John William Johnson and Johanna Simmons were born on Saba, and her maternal grandfather William was born on St. Michaels, Barbados and so on.

Capt. Cameron Dudley Simmons (left) and his son Capt. Sydney Augustus Simmons, with the rest of his family in a family portrait (1944)

Captain Cameron Dudley Simmons was born on Saba July 10th, 1892 and died on January 17th, 1945 in the Pacific Ocean.

Dudley and his brother Samuel left Saba as young men on a schooner, sailing between the Caribbean islands and New York. After sailing as mate on the schooner he then sailed steam ships with the American Hawaiian Line until he received his Master's license. He sailed as Master on tankers and freighters. Some of the vessels which he commanded were the tankers SS *Antietam*, SS *Bulkco*, SS *E. J. Nicholas* and the freighters SS *Alamar*, SS *Cubore*.

The story of the voyages to Murmansk is one of almost unbelievable horror, or matchless courage, and of unlimited devotion to duty. There is nothing quite like it in all history. Ships, which left the ports of the United States for Russia, had about only 33% chance of returning. If struck by enemy forces, chances of rescue from sinking ships in sub-zero weather were slim to none, in spite of all efforts to save personnel whenever possible. Even if there was no incident, the long watches in severe sub-cero temperatures, multiplied by strong gusts of sea breeze made the trip one of the most trying experiences imaginable. Few men could stand the strain of many trips to Murmansk. The Maritime Commission indicates that 6,989 members of the Merchant Marine became causalities, either dead or missing, during WW II. Over 580 were made prisoners. The military commanders of both the United States and her Allies testified repeatedly to the high value of the contribution merchant ships and merchant seamen made toward ultimate victory.

The first merchant ship to make the eastbound convoy to North Russia (PQ-8 out of Iceland) with a Navy Armed Guard was the 3800-ton freighter SS *Larranga*. At the insistence of Captain Cameron Dudley Simmons, she was installed with a Navy Armed Guard contingent consisting of Ensign H. A. Axtell, Jr. and eight enlisted men under his supervision. The ordnance placed on the SS *Larranga* was one 4-inch gun and eight 30-calibre machine guns. The Armed Guard crew of this ship had the distinction of being the first to fire on an enemy submarine from an armed merchant vessel.

On December 6, 1941, the SS *Larranga* left the port of Boston on a trip that ultimately took her to Murmansk. The staff of Armed Guard got their first taste of battle when it fired three rounds at a surfaced submarine on Christmas Eve, perhaps scoring a hit on the second round.

The ship also received a hit, but retained watertight integrity and went into Reykjavik for repairs. Captain Simmons went ashore but when returning to the ship on a launch he was injured when his leg was between the ship and the dock. He was hospitalized for approximately three months due to a severe foot injury. When the ship returned from Murmansk, it put into Reykjavik for him.

In July 1942, he assumed command of the SS *William Wirt*, launched with two other Liberty Ships on July 4 of that same year.

The ship loaded in Newport News, Virginia and August 1 set sail for the United Kingdom, arriving in Avonmouth, England. After discharging cargo, the ship proceeded to Newport, Wales to await loading for the North African invasion in November. The SS "*William Wirt*" was the first ship to enter a North African port during the invasion.

In January 1943, navigating from Liverpool to Phillipeville, Algeria the SS 'William Wirt', under the command of Captain Simmons, was subjected to four separate enemy bombing attacks while operating, in convoy, in the Mediterranean Sea. Her cargo consisted of a lethal mix of 16,000 drums of high-octane airplane fuel and several thousand cases of TNT. She was attacked by German torpedo and dive-bombers. The Armed Guard aboard the Liberty ship opened fire and was able to shoot down several planes. As one of the planes flew toward portside machine gun strafe from the ship ripped off one of its engines, bursting into flames. The plane banked and dropped its bombs before going under water, and one of them struck the ship at the No. 1 hold, about 4 ft above the water line. The bomb penetrated the ship and landed amongst the gasoline drums and cases of TNT in the No. 1 hold, yet failed to explode. The savvy crew was able to maintain tight water management and the ship managed to reach Phillipsville two days later where the bomb was disabled and cargo discharged.

It was the first experience in action for the majority of Merchant Seamen stationed as members of the gun crews, but they worked their guns as seasoned veterans. Several planes were shot down and many others were damaged or driven off. This excellent performance was due, in large measure to the skillful training and indoctrination by Captain Simmons and the Chief Mate Holm who were also responsible for the high state of morale prevailing in the ship's company. In addition the Master displayed expert judgment and ability in maneuvering his ship to provide maximum advantage to the battery. His calm, courageous and efficient handling of the situation contributed greatly to the defeat of the enemy and was a lasting inspiration to all seamen of the United States Merchant Marine.

The following official report of the Navy Department concerns the Liberty cargo ship SS *"William Wirt,"* with Capt. Cameron Dudley Simmons and Chief Mate George Irvin Holm at the helm. The report was compiled by the Commander of U.S. Naval Armed Guard "SS *William Wirt*," from Gibraltar, directed to the chief of Naval Operations and dated February 2nd, 1943. There were 21 armed guards on board under the command of Lieut. R.H. Mcilwaine. The merchant personnel consisted of 13 merchant men assigned to gun posts, among them Capt. Samuel Augustus Simmons Jr. (brother of the Captain) and listed as Third Mate. There was also a Jones, M. L., Peterson, M. C., Green, J. H. and Collins, J.

P. (Third cook). These are all Saba names and they could have been from here as our people liked to sail together even into war. The report is of the Voyage of the SS *"William Wirt"* from December 28th, 1943 to January 10th, 1944.

On 7 January 1943, approximately seventy miles West of Philippeville Algeria, we encountered the enemy. With no warning whatsoever from escorts, an attack by air was launched against the convoy at 1810. Planes painted dark grey, with no visible insignias, came in from the North, North East and North West. Flying low, about 50 to 100 feet above the water, the first assault was launched by torpedo carrying planes. The ship on our portside was the first to go up with a great explosion, which destroyed the attacking plane that was caught and sucked into the flame. Simultaneously, torpedo planes came in on our port bow and quarter. 3"/50 and 20MM Oerlikon barrage drove these planes off their course causing their torpedoes to go astray. Another followed close, coming in on the port quarter and was hit by 20MM fire. He dropped two torpedoes, one going astray and the other hitting a small Norwegian ship astern sinking her, then burst into flames and fell to our starboard side aft. The next wave, followed closely and were dive bombers coming in high from North or seaside. One diving on us on the port beam was hit by 20MM fire and his port motor burst into flames, causing him to bank sharply to port and the two bombs released to fall twenty yards from the portside of the ship. He appeared to try and gain altitude, then released another bomb which entered No. 1 hold (Loaded with 100 octane gas); and fell into drink just forward of our starboard bow. The explosion of the two near misses jammed the breech and training arc of the 3"/50 and we had to carry on with 20MM alone. The last wave of planes approached from forward and crossed our bow. One was hit by 20MM from flying bridge starboard and rapidly lost altitude with heavy black smoke pouring from his motors. He fell into the drink about one mile astern.

The actual attack ended at 1850 and approximately twenty or more planes were used by the enemy. These consisted, to the best of our ability to recognize them, of Heinkles, Folke-Wulf, Stuka and Junkers bombers. Also, some planes resembling Savia SM's.

The attack, we feel, was the result of a reconnaissance plane which appeared over the convoy at 1605. Escorting Hurricanes opened fire and the plane disappeared into a cloud with no pursuit attempted. Two hours and five minutes later the actual attack occurred, at which time no warning and very little support was given to the convoy by sea escorts.

Shrapnel and some unexploded shells fell on deck and hatch covers but no injuries except minor ones were received. The bomb entering No.1 hold did not set off the gasoline; it was removed in pieces after arrival at Philipeville. Our next encounter took place on the return, westerly course, on 19 January 1943; planes approached low over the water from North and seaside. All batteries ordered to open fire and barrage diverted the planes from their course. The next wave of attacking planes came in on the port bow. 3'/50 and 20MM barrage hit one plane and dispersed the others who retreated flying to northward. The last attack came from high-level bombers, but no hits on the ships were scored.

At 1305 escort hoisted his black pennant and began dropping depth charges on our starboard side abaft the beam. At about 1320 an enemy sub surfaced and was fired on and sank immediately by escort. Escort put over life raft and the convoy steamed on, proceeding west.

Another attack was encountered on January 20th. And a second attack about six hours out of Algiers on that same date. At 2045, and again with no warning and very little support from our sea escort, the attack was launched against the convoy. This action lasted for one hour and five minutes and was our last encounter before anchoring at Gibraltar. Every man in the crew, including signalman H.F. Wilson, stayed by his station throughout the night, each night of the attacks. All were calm, determined and relentless in their persecution of the enemy. Even after a bomb had entered No.1 hold (containing 100 octane gas) and none knew when an explosion might mean the ship's destruction, all hands remained at the gun stations throughout the night. Every man asked only the chance to further protect his ship and help her make port and deliver the cargo.

Further commendation is due to the merchant personnel assisting in servicing the guns. Nothing but the highest praise can be offered for them too. Like gunners, they too, exhibited a calm determination to eradicate any and all enemy within sight, no matter what cost. The Master, C. D. Simmons, and Chief Mate G. I. Holm, did their utmost in navigating safely and presenting the best fighting point of vantage for the ship. Too, Chief mate G. I. Holm did more than anyone to prevent panic. With no thought of himself he jollied and kidded his men and by doing so preserved order and discipline so necessary in such times of crisis." The office of the chief of naval operations also made a report which stated that the SS *William Wirt* was damaged as the result of a series of air attacks. She had sailed from Liverpool in a convoy which consisted of 13 merchant ships and 5 escort vessels. Although damaged, the ship made port safely and returned to the USA where it underwent repairs.

For the Algiers mission Capt. Simmons was awarded the Medal for Meritorious Service. He was later the Commander of another Liberty ship until sometime in the spring of 1944 when he became captain of the *SS Point Loma*, a seagoing tugboat.

Keeping in touch with family in such remote places and not knowing ahead of time where the next mission would be was not an easy task, as reflected in a letter to his daughter Marjorie dated February 25, 1944: "I received your letter; it chased me around quite a lot but eventually caught up with me. Have had a long trip but eventually got here and delivered the goods which is all that is expected. Sorry to say that it will be a while yet before I will be coming home as they are sending me a little further on , but what's a thousand miles or more in your old man's young life. It's just that more to add to the thousands I have already traveled in the pass thirty seven years."

Dark humor was also included in his lines "… I will keep on going as long as I can stand on my foot and a half" in a clear reference to his accident. "… and after that I will sit home with you, and if I give you too much trouble, there is always 'Snug Harbor'" in reference to the well-known Old Sailor's retirement home.

He would ask in his letters to "remember me to Marie, Sydney and the rest. Sorry I was the only one missing for xmas. Maybe next year."

He served on the *SS "Point Loma"* in the War of the Pacific until his death in January 1945. Here is the log report on his death at sea, a fate suffered by so many Sabans in former times.

- January 15th, 1945, Monday; Purser was called to Captain's cabin. He was complaining of dizziness. At once he passed out. Artificial respiration was begun. Signalman called for Doctor who was brought alongside by Navy tug. At about 1525 doctor pronounced captain dead of heart attack, which occurred at 1350.

- January 16th, Tuesday 1815: Gun crew formed guard of Honor for sea burial. First-Mate Kelly read short services. He [the Captain] slipped from under flag and was confined to the sea at 18:30. And so, Captain Cameron Dudley Simmons found a watery grave in that vast Pacific Ocean.

He ended his career as so many from Saba did back then. He was buried at sea on January 16, 1945 (LAT 02 DEG 29 MIN N LONG 153 DEG 50 MIN W), approximately 600 miles north of the Solomon Island of New Ireland.

The movie film *"Action in the North Atlantic"*, issued in 1943 and featuring Humphrey Bogart, Raymond Massey, and Alan Hale, portrayed the actions of ships like the *SS Larange* and its crew, and illustrated the importance of the Naval Armed Guard and how it interfaced with the Merchant Marine crew who were in charge of their vessel. As the tagline for the movie says, *"a thunderous story of the men of the merchant marine"*!

Joseph Horton 'Redhead Joe' Simmons Jr.

Joseph Horton Simmons Jr. was the oldest son of Joseph Horton Simmons Sr. (1823-1901) and Mary Catherine Davis (1828-1879), born on Saba on March 25th 1861; his siblings were James Allen and James Anthony Simmons.

There were two merchants from The Bottom named Joseph Simmons. He was known as "Redhead Joe" to differentiate him from Joseph Benjamin Simmons, aka as "Blackhead Joe" who also became a prominent merchant.

The schooner *"The Ethel"* was owned by "Redhead Joe" Simmons and the Captain was Willie Hassell. Their regular port of call was St. Kitts which they would visit two or three times a week. The sloop *"Muriel,"* which belonged to Capt. John Simmons, also used to trade with St. Thomas.

In hurricane season, these ships would go to St. Barths, along with two large rowboats, the *"Challenge"* and the *"Surprise"*, which also belonged to "Redhead Joe" Simmons. In any event, when a hurricane threatened, most of these boats could be hauled up on land, loaded up with rocks, and thus weather the storm out.

Joseph Simmons was part of the Sabans which at a given time pursued fortune on other islands. He died on Barbados.

Engle Herbert Heyliger

Engle Herbert Heyliger was born on February 10, 1900. He was the third child born to Engle Heyliger and Amalia Every. He was lost at sea off the coast of North Carolina, aboard SS Cassimir on February 26, 1942.

The freighter SS Cassimir, owned by the Cuba Distilling Co. Inc. of New York, transported molasses from Baltimore to Cuba to be used in the rum making process. On the morning of February 26, 1942, the Cassimir was moving through a dense fog about 50 miles east of the tip of Frying Pan Shoals. Due to the heavy U-boat reports in the area, the Cassimer was traveling at full speed and most likely under radio silence.

Also, moving through the fog was the freighter, SS Lara. The ships were unable to change course and the bow of the Lara cut a gash into the starboard side of the Cassimir at amidships. Lifeboats were launched and 32 members of the crew were to be later rescued by the SS Lara, although one, Chief Officer Engle Heyliger (age 41) was to soon die from his injuries.

William James Benjamin 'Ben' Hassell

He was the fourth child of William James Benjamin Hassell (1840-1924) and his wife Elizabeth Hassell (1843-1924), born on about 1863 on Saba. He married Mary Love Hassell, a daughter of Lovelock Hassell and Agnes Holm. His siblings were Richard Roland, John George, Abraham Heyliger, John Clarence, George, Thomas, Angeline, Carl and Lena Hassell. As many Sabans of the day, Capt. 'Ben' Hassell moved with his family from Windwardside, Saba to Barbados about 1911.

In his lifetime he owned many large trading schooners: Lovely Lila, Columbia, Maise Hassell, Dutch Princess, John H. Hassell, Three Sisters. Other Schooners owned by Captain Hassell were: 'Margie Turner', 'Olympic', 'Love and Loulou', 'Indusrie', 'Carib', 'Daisy', 'Wild Rover', 'Edward VII', 'Nathaniel L. Gordon', 'Priscilla', 'Nicola', 'Zurah', 'Mary Love', 'Rhode Island', 'Peerless', 'Delphine Cabral', 'Mona Marie', 'Agnes', and the 'Lasca'.

The 'Lasca' was a yacht owned by German Kaiser Wilhelm's son and was purchased from the British after the German capitulation at the end of World War I.

The schooner 'Mary Love Hassell', owned by Captain Ben, sailed from St. Kitts on April 28th 1896 bound for New York, and made it there in twelve sailing days. His 105 ton 'Esther Anita' made a record run from New York to Saba in nine days.

The 'Zurah' was navigated from Rhode Island to Saba by Bernard Leverock during the month of May 1919. Captain Ben owned more than twenty schooners during his lifetime. He died in 1933 and was buried in Barbados.

His brother Abraham used to buy schooners in Maine and the East Coast, and bring them down for the West Indies trade. On Barbados the Sabans gradually established themselves as boat builders and large trading schooners which provided the main source of transportation between Barbados and the other Caribbean islands.

Ida, one of Captain Ben's daughters, married a Mr. Bruce Goddard who owned Goddard Enterprises, with many investments in real estate, supermarkets, hotels, import-export and shipping interests throughout the West Indies. Their son Richard now runs the business empire. A daughter Betty Lee, married the famous cricket player.

Theophilus Wilson

He was born on November 3rd 1910 and married to Clothilda Rosina Horton Cornet with whom he had Moceta Ulean Wilson.

Theo worked as a Sailor aboard the oil tanker Hermes, owned by the Anglo Saxon Petroleum Co.

I'm not certain of the circumstances but he died at Haifa, Israel on 31 December 1941 and was buried at the Sharon Civil Cemetery, Haifa (Israel)

Edward Austin Simmons

He was the son of Edward James 'Ebbie' Simmons Sr. (1846-1905) and Josephine Simmons (1848-1910), born on Saba on July 9th 1873. He was part of a large family of eight which included Blanche, Carl Heyliger, Henry 'Harry', Ida Clementina, Edward James Jr., and Josephine 'Josie' Simmons. He married into another family of sailors when he married Joanna Leverock 'Baby' Vanterpool, -a daughter of Capt. Ernest Hugh Toland Vanterpool (1852-1919) and Elizabeth Simmons Leverock Winfield (1862-1905)-, on December 20th 1905. They had two children: Rev. Alvin Edward Simmons and Hubert 'Bertie' Vanterpool Simmons.

Edward was the Second Mate of the SS Korona. On the Manifest of Aliens employed on the vessel as members of the crew arriving New York on Feb. 23, 1918 he is described as: AGE:42; Sex: M; Race: USA; Nationality: Dutch; Height: 5.6 1/2; Weight: 152; Physical marks: None

As a very busy seaman, Austin spent much of his time away from the island, so even after his marriage to Joanna, she did not move into her new home but rather stayed at her paternal home and that was where his first son was born. This afforded Alvin a solid foundation under the training of his mother and her two sisters: Estelle and Blanch, who were very active Christian church workers and took the young Alvin with them on their many church missions. Eventually this became the foundation of his calling to the priesthood.

Austin was naturalized at the Supreme Court of Brooklyn, NY on the 18th of July 1900.

William Simmons Barnes

He was the oldest son of Richard Henry Barnes (1858-1916) and Ada Isabel Hassell (1869-1906), born June 30th 1895 on Saba. Other siblings were Anthonius, Lillian Pearl and Peter Willem Barnes. Capt. William Barnes married to Daisy Hutson King and has one daughter: Madeline.

Hubert Lovelace Hassell

Capt. Hubert L. Hassell

With the exception of his sister Clemencia, Hubert came from a family of all sea captains. He was the youngest son of William Lovelace Hassell and Emeline Every, born on November 2, 1896 on Saba and died on July 2, 1968 in San Leadro, CA. His siblings were Capt. John William 'Whippie' Hassell, Capt. Peter John Hassell, and Capt. James 'Jim' Hassell.

Captain Hubert L. Hassell entered the Company's employ as a third mate on April 11th, 1924 and was continuously Captain since June 8, 1936. He was a Lieutenant Commander in the Naval Reserve from January 22, 1941 and was granted leave of absence on August 2nd 1943, for active service in the Navy.

Many Saban captains had an active participation in WW II, if not in a battlefield with armored ships, as merchant marines transporting goods to the warfront. However, on the coastline there had also been several scrimmages with German U-Boats. Such was the case of Captain Hubert Hassell and his most intense adventure as described in the book "Torpedo Junction: U-Boat War Off America's East Coast." (Hickam, 1996)

While navigating "lights-out" in a pitched-black night, the SS E. M. Clark, a 9647 ton tanker owned by Standard Oil of New Jersey, carrying 188,725 barrels of heating oil loaded at Baton Rouge and bound for New York, was sailing on a course required to take her safely past the deadly shoals marked by the "Diamond Shoals" lighted buoy. Unfortunately her silhouette was drawn in the horizon by a typical Hatteras-style thunderstorm and spotted by a U-Boat (U-124) commanded by the famed KaptainLeutnant Johann Mohr (a.k.a "The Grey Wolf") at 01:35 on March 18, 1942.

Captain Hassell was in bed when a loud thump made the ship tremble. As he reached the bridge he learned of the damage report of a large port side hole. Realizing that an emergency signal had to be sent, he immediately ran to the radio room. The operator reported that there was damage to the main antenna so they tried to cobble together a solution. However, as they were about to hookup the makeshift antenna the ship was impacted by a second torpedo. Captain Hassell had no alternative than to order "Abandon Ship" to all hands without being able to send the SOS signal.

Captain Hassell left the ship only after he had taken a head count sure that all hands were accounted for except utility-man Thomas Larkin, who had been asleep in the hospital room in the vicinity of the first torpedo explosion and was presumed dead, he climbed into the number 1 boat. Struggling against both wind and sea, the two small life boats had just gotten clear of the big hull when a sailor was spotted still aboard the sinking vessel, standing at her rail. Captain Hassell directed his boat to pull half-way back to the tanker, then shouted for the seaman to jump overboard. They recovered the last seaman, and rowed to the open sea.

Luckily for them the ship's stern lifted high and the tanker plunged slowly forward and down which must have kept the U-Boat from returning to look and dispose of any survivors. At the first signs of light, several ships were spotted in the horizon. Captain Hassell shot two red flares and caught the attention of the destroyer *Dickerson* who was hunting for a killer U-Boat responsible for sinking the evening before the *Acme* and the *Kassandra Louloudis*, and now the *E. M. Clark*, but only finding its survivors. Of the 41 officers and men aboard the E. M. Clark that night, the only life lost was that of Thomas J. Larkin.

Capt. Hassell was immediately transferred to another tanker and on May 28th 1942, a week before the battle of Midway, the ESSO tanker "E.T. Bedford", (sister ship of the "E.M. Clark" and 516.6 feet long) arrived at Sydney, Australia, with 95,195 barrels of 100 octane aviation gasoline and 20, 646 barrels of Pool vaporizing oil or a total cargo of one hundred and fifteen thousand and forty one barrels of refined petroleum products[8]. This cargo was delivered to the Commonwealth of Australia during the most serious crisis in her history, when she was threatened by the onrushing land, sea, and air forces of Japan. The tanker was commanded by Captain Hubert L. Hassell and her engine room was in charge of Chief Engineer Ervin C. Haatveldt. The vitally important cargo was discharged at five terminals. Four midget Japanese submarines entered Sydney Harbor and attempted to blow up the "E.T. Bedford" but they were detected by the cruiser "USS Chicago". General MacArthur's headquarters announced that all four subs were destroyed, but that 19 Australian sailors were killed and 10 injured on the ferryboat- the only Allied vessel lost.

On the night of May 31, during the enemy submarine raid, the "E.T. Bedford" was shaken and damaged by the concussion of depth charges which were dropped near the ship and she afterwards showed signs of leaks in her hull plates. At first the leaks were not considered important, but later the damage was found to be serious. After loading a small cargo, 20, 146 barrels of 73-octane gasoline at Sydney and discharging at Towns-Ville, Australia, the "E.T. Bedford" sailed across the Pacific to San Francisco, where she arrived on June 27. Repairs to hull and engines took considerable time; it was 5 months and 26 days before she re-entered service on December 22nd.

Captain Hubert Lovelace Hassell retired from Standard Oil in 1966 and passed away in 1969. In 1970 the ancestral home on St. John's of this particular Hassell family was sold and the family passed into history.

---

[8] Auke Visser's International Esso Tankers site
(http://www.aukevisser.nl/inter/id766.htm)

James 'Jim' Hassell

He was born to a family of seafaring siblings. He was the fourth child of William Lovelace Hassell (1843-1899) and Emeline Every. His siblings were Clemencia, John William, Peter John and Hubert Lovelace. He was born on November 7th 1889, captain of merchant freighters, who married Amy Leverock a daughter John George Hassell Leverock (1852-1931) and Catherine Kelly Winfield.

On June 5th 1917, he enlisted in South Boston, MA for WW I as Mariner when he was working for Standard Oil Co.

He was a merchant marine serving mostly on freighters. He sailed twice to Murmansk, Russia in a supply convoy in WW II while with the merchant marines. Served as the XO (Lieutenant) in WW II on navy transport vessels.

He became what sailors called a "landlubber;" in 1940 it seems he had retired from sea faring life, as his occupation is listed as Painter in the 1940 census at 50 years old. He retired in 1968 to Florida and died on December 3rd 1970 at ST. Petersburg, FL

Peter John Hassell

Born May 17th 1883. Capt. Peter was married to Floria Mathilde Every, who later, after Peter died, married Joseph E. Vlaun. He was a son of William Lovelace Hassell (1843-1899) and Emeline Every (1855-1926). Peter died at the age of 50 in 1934 just a few years after he mastered his own ship.

Lloyd Every

Capt. Lloyd Every of Saba/Barbados at the helm of the large Saban owned schooner *"Marion Belle Wolfe"* which sailed out of Barbados to the rest of the West Indies for more than 30 years.

She was a large Grand Banks two-masted schooner built to withstand the rough weather of the Atlantic Ocean for several weeks and then sail home fast with a full cargo of cod to reach the market in the shortest possible time. It was built in Shelburne, Nova Scotia, Canada in 1920, had a length of 126 feet (38.4m) long and a registered tonnage of 116 tons.

After ending her Grand Banks fishing career, the Marion Belle Wolfe was converted to the Caribbean trade, being based initially in Saba, Netherlands West Indies, under the command of Captain Will Leverock.

John William 'Whippy' Hassell

Captain of steamers was born on Saba on October 16th 1890. He was the second child born to a seafaring family of William Lovelace Hassell (1843 - 1899) and Emeline Every (1855 – 1926). His siblings were Clemencia, Peter John, James and Hubert Lovelace Hassell.

He died August 8th 1962 on Saint John's Village on Saba.

John Alfred 'Johnny' Leverock

John Alfred Leverock, better known in his circles as "Johnny," was born in St. John's Village, Saba, Dutch West Indies on Apr 5th 1901. He was the oldest of 13 children born to John Leverock (1876-1962) and Alice Hassell (1879-xxxx). His siblings were Rita, Eunice, Eleanor Pearl, Enid, George Nathaniel, James, Charles Irvin, Alice Catherine, Violet, Hubert Lovelace, Doris Ethel, and Thomas.

A sailor most of his life, he left his beloved Saba for the first time as a cabin boy at the age of 10, on a schooner where he would learn and build up his marine skills. He arrived to stay in the United States on June 16th 1917 at the young age of 16 years and 2 months aboard the SS Prince Willem I and used Mr. Kaliski's address as the "Seaman's Institute". He served in both World Wars, and the Korean War. Before WW II he was an aviator in the Flying Circus. By the end of the conflict he was commissioned a Commander in the Merchant Marine, internationally licensed to command any ship in the world. He was on the merchant ships SS Muskogee, SS Swiftscout, the SS John Hay and the SS Central Victory among others.

He met his wife Bertha Catherine Habraken while he was working at the aerial circus in Ohio, whom he married on Mar 3rd, 1924. They had four children: Alice, Marguerite, John Alfred and Richard.

He became a mechanic and owned a paint and body shop which he worked with his children. As the story goes, during a poker game, Johnny won a "perpetual lease" for seven acres of Tampa Bay oyster beds. He began to cultivate oysters and soon needed an outlet for his annual 15,000 bushel harvest. Consequently, in 1948, he opened Johnny Leverock's Oyster Bar in Pinellas Park, FL. This early eating establishment was a single room with one large stone table and a few benches. Patrons shucked the oysters themselves and tossed the shells through a hole in the middle of the table.

Johnny Leverock with his trademark Saban hat, surrounded by wife Bertha and three of their children

The restaurant soon flourished and became the gathering place for public figures, visitors and locals alike. He later added rooms to accommodate his growing business. It was in this restaurant that Johnny and other community leaders founded the Florida Sheriff's Youth Ranch, which has grown to several locations around the State of Florida. His annual Fish Frying was a strong fund raiser for the farm and by 2013 it is still one of its major benefactors.

Johnny's wife Bertha, developed special recipes for fresh grouper, hushes puppies and other delicacies. Her famous Clam Chowder, Key Lime Pie and Peanut Butter Pie were still being served at all the Leverock's Restaurants which they sold in 1980's. Her celebrated 'wet batter' recipe was used on their famous golden fried shrimp.

Their Restaurant's tagline was a reflection of the candid Saban Ways: *"Remember, if it's fresher than Leverock's, it's still swimming!"*

Always an active participant of the Pinellas county community, he was a member of the St. Giles Episcopal Church, Master Mates Pilots of America, Lealman Lions Club, and a life member of Moose Lodge 1145 and the Florida Sheriffs Association.

He died peacefully at his residence at Pinellas Park, FL on April 9th 1976.

Joseph Hassell

Joseph came from a large family of fourteen children. He was the sixth, born on July 3, 1890 to Simon Hassell (1858-1909) and Eliza Jane Wilson. He relied on his seaman skills he learned on his native Saba to enlist in WW I as an able body seaman.

He worked as an Able Body seaman working for the J. S. Emery Shipping Co, aboard the SS Tifton, the Ella Pierce Thurlow and the SS Orizaba amongst others.

At 52 years of age he enlisted again for WW II and listed one Christine Horton as his emergency contact. We suspect this is the daughter of David Wright Horton (1849-1931) and Eliza Woods (1855-1931).

Abraham Heyliger 'Abe' Hassell

Born August 19th 1866 in Saba, Capt. Hassell grew up with the sea, worked on it as a cabin boy and continued his love of it when he came to the United States as a young man. He was the third child born to the couple of William James Benjamin Hassell (1841-1924) and Elizabeth Hassell (1843-1924). His siblings were Richard Roland, John George, William James Benjamin Jr., John Clarence, George, Thomas, Angeline, Lena and Carle Hassell.

Capt. Abraham Hassell, who for more than 25 years found purchasing and retrofitting vessels in the US for resale in the West Indies and the Caribbean area to be highly profitable, died at Newport Hospital after a long illness at the age of 89.

His great commercial success started in 1906, when he bought the schooner *"Frolic,"* which had been impounded by the government for illegal use in the transportation of Chinese citizens from Cuba to America. He sold the ship for striking profits in Cayenne, French Guyana which jumpstarted his business career.

With his keen eye, over the next twenty-five years he bought various schooners which he had repaired and refitted at Gloucester, Mass., reselling them in Puerto Rico, Barbados and the Virgin Islands. One of the schooners he sold was the *"Virginia"* built at the Herreschoff Shipyard in Bristol, Mass.

For four years, Capt. Hassell sailed the three-masted schooner *"Francis and Louise"* trading among the Antilles Islands. He also bought the sloop *"Fairwind"* which had been hauled out on the beach at East Greenwich for three years, shined up, and then shipped off to the fishing grounds for cod around Block Island, using a nor'west breeze with all canvas set and drawing well. Though the sloop was 40 feet on deck, with a beam of 13 feet, it seemed to Abe rather "small potatoes" when compared to the vessels he had taken out to the West Indies.

By his own accord, the schooner yacht *"Viking"* was the prettiest ship he ever owned, yet it had also brought him his only disaster; the schooner went down in a storm off the Virgin Islands, a total wreck, however all hands were saved. Capt. Hassell's last venture at sea was in 1931, after which he decided it was time to retire.

For most of his working life, Capt. Hassell lived in Providence, RI moving to Newport in 1947 to live with a daughter Florencia Lulu Hassell-Nolan, when he became seriously ill and finally died in 1955. He left another daughter, Mrs. Adele Hassell Gannon of Newport; a granddaughter and one great granddaughter. He was preceded in death by his wife Caroline Hassell (1909), and his daughters Carrie Louise (1896) and Ruth (1953).

John William 'Dow' Dowling

He was born on Dec 24th 1894, the first born child to John William Dowling (1865-1936) and Mary Elizabeth Hassell (1872-1909); his siblings were Aldrick, Wadron and Ruby. On January 20 1921 he married to Annie Barnes, a daughter of Amadis Lubencio Barnes (1864-1910) and Rosella Kelly (1870-1896). They established in Providence, RI where they had a daughter, Cynthia.

He enlisted for WW I as a Third-Mate on May 27th, 1918 giving the address of Hyman Kaliski in New York as his US address. It seems he was quite determined and eager to help in this war because he also enlisted in Puerto Rico on June 21st 1917 most likely when his ship was at that Port of Call. In 1922 he came to NY to visit his brother Waldron at Richmond Hill. He also listed as an emergency contact his Uncle Capt. James Hassell, living at the time in St. Thomas, VI.

Thomas Charles Vanterpool

Thomas Charles Vanterpool was the youngest son of the marriage of Thomas Charleswell Vanterpool (1826-1880) and Johanna 'Hannah' Simmons, a daughter of Abraham 'Braw' Simmons and his wife Elizabeth 'Mam' Horton. All of his brothers, -Ernest Hugh Toland & Johnny Pitman Vanterpool-, became captains and owners of large schooners which traded between the West Indies and New York.

Thomas Charles Vanterpool

Captain Tommy used to own the home which is now the residence of the Lt. Governor of Saba. He also owned a large number of schooners in his lifetime. The largest was the 'Mayflower' which was 147 feet long and weighed 190.27 tons. This schooner was built in Gloucester, Mass., to compete in the "Bluenose" races.

The schooner 'Lena Vanterpool' once saved the life of her master, Captain Tommy. As the story goes he used to smuggle-out escaped convicts from Cayenne who paid their passage in gold nuggets gathered from the rivers of French Guyana. An old black woman on shore used to signal the Captain when prisoners were ready to board. On that particular night, the old lady signaled imminent danger. Captain Tommy did not wait to pull up the anchor, but ordered it cast away when he spied a French Man-Of-War rounding the point and coming in his direction. It is claimed that the 'Lena Vanterpool' sailed so fast that when she reached Barbados the oakum had been washed out of her seams.

At one point when the French Man-Of-War was getting too close for comfort the captain ordered more sail and pleased with his schooner "Go Lena go, your master is in trouble. Spread your wings and fly like an eagle." He had ordered the crew if the French caught up with them to put him in a barrel and throw him overboard.

Ernest Hugh Toland Vanterpool

The family: (back) Capt. Ernest Hugh Toland Vanterpool, Estelle, Johanna, Blanche, Austin Simmons, (front) Hubert, Charles Pittman and Donald Vanterpool.

He was the oldest son of Thomas Charles Vanterpool (1826-1880) and Johanna 'Hanna' Simmons (1829-1879), born on Saba February 1st 1852.

He married Elizabeth Simmons Winfield Leverock 1862-1905) a daughter of Governor Moses Leverock and his wife Mary Ann 'Mammie' Winfield. Her surname was that of her father, the 'Winfield' that of her mother and the 'Simmons' that of her grandmother (wife of Governor Edward Beaks). The former first families of The Bottom had this custom in order to clearly determine the relationships between the various families.

Captain Ernest and his brother Captain "Tommy" (Charles Thomas Vanterpool) were considered among the wealthiest Captains of their time. Reportedly they always requested payment in gold and the latter brother was almost caught once by a French Man-O-War. Captain Ernest sent an emissary with a sealed galvanize pail to bring to his house in The Bottom. When the wife saw the pail she said: "I cannot believe this. Another pail of gold! What does Ernest intend to do with all this gold. The ceiling is full and under all the beds is full. I have to remind him that you cannot eat gold." His descendants claim that it must have been a tall tale as they certainly knew nothing about him having any gold much less the amount claimed by his fellow islanders.

After a fruitful life, he died on March 19th 1919 at the Bottom, on Saba.

Peter John Hassell Dowling

Born on Saba on August 7th 1893, was a son of Peter John Hassell Dowling (1864-1917) and Johanna Lovelace Hassell (1870-1946). In the early 1920's he married Rita Leverock, a daughter of John Leverock (1876-1962) and Alice Hassell (1879-xxxx), both from Saba. His mother

Johanna is listed in the NY State Census of 1925 as living with them at 13th St in Brooklyn.

Together, they had nine children: Rita, Peter, Johanna, George, Irvin Dowling, Stanley, John "Jackie", Bertha and Beulah Dowling. He enlisted as a Seaman/Officer for WW I on Sept 6th 1917. He also enlisted for WW II while working at Maritime Company out of NYC. In December 1945 he was working with Luckenbach Shipping Co, and was the Master of the merchant ship /troop transport SS Kemp P. Battle arriving from Le Havre, France which saw action in the Mediterranean Convoys of April 1944 credited with one plane kill. He was also the Master for the SS Henry T Rainey. He died about April 1958.

Charles Pitman Vanterpool

A son of Capt. Ernest Hugh Toland Vanterpool (1852-1919) and Elizabeth Simmons Winfield Leverock (1862-1905), Charles was born on Saba on July 26th 1894. His siblings were: Johanna 'Baby', William Donald, Ernest Hubert, Estelle, Blanche, and Dora Vanterpool.

He navigated as a Third-Mate aboard ships such as the SS Maracaibo commanded by his second cousin, also from Saba, Capt. Evan Lambert Simmons.

He arrived to the USA in 1912 and was naturalized by the Southern District Court of New York on August 21st 1917, living at 2618 Avenue N, Brooklyn, NY. He enlisted for WW I in 1917, where he reached the rank of Lieutenant, commissioned aboard the ships Lake Ontario and Manhattan.

He is listed as the First Mate aboard the SS Milwaukee Bridge in 1921 working for Moore & McCormack with Allen Otis Simmons (son of "Red Head Joe" Simmons) working as a fireman. He was also the Second Mate of the SS Santa Cecilia working for Planet Shipping Co in 1925. He worked for the Red "D" Line in their Caribbean routes to Curacao, Cuba, Puerto Rico, Venezuela and other destinations aboard ships such as SS Tachira, SS Zulia, SS Caracas and SS Carabobo.

Charles Pitman Vanterpool

From records we have apparently identified he married twice; first to one Gertrude Flynn. In his WW II registration card and in the 1925 New York State census he appears married to Dorothy Tucker which might coincide with a marriage record subscribed in New York on May 28th 1921.

He died at the age of 89 on January 8th 1984 at Northampton, Hamptonshire Co., MA.

Abram Thomas Mardenborough

Capt. Abram Thomas Mardenborough was the third child born about 1866 to the marriage of Abram Thomas Desmond Peterson Mardenborough (1825-1906) and Sarah Leverock (1837-1921). His siblings were: Adeline, Cordelia, Peter and Lillian Mardenborough. He married Ina Marie Johnson (1874-1921), a daughter of Henry Hassell 'Buddy' Johnson (1835-1920) and Ann Rebecca Hassell (1842-1917) on January 23rd 1896 and they had three children: Ulric, Claude Wilfred and Elliot Elmore Mardenborough.

The schooner "Virginia" belonged to Captain Abraham Mardenborough of Windwardside. The schooner was built on Curacao. It serviced the Dutch Windward Islands, St. Kitts and St. Thomas. He had a contract with the government to transport passengers and mail between these islands in the 1920's.

After the death of his first wife, Capt. Mardenborough married to Mary Ann "Miss Ohney" Wathey, daughter of John Joseph Wathey (1859-1918) and Anna Paulina Williams (1858-1936) of St. Maarten. She was his second wife by whom he had no children. He lived on Frontstreet in Philipsburg.

He died at the age of 84 on January 17th 1951 in Sint Maarten.

John George Hassell Leverock Jr.

He was the second child born at the village of St. John's, Saba on August 21st 1881 to the family of John George Hassell Leverock Sr. (1852-1931) and Catherine Kelly Winfield, who had a total of eight children: Susan Laura, Ann Rebecca, Thomas Aubrey, Edmund Wilfred 'Will', Amy, Evelyn 'Evie' and Bernard 'Ben' Leverock.

He became Merchant Marine Captain and married to Victoria Hassell (1887-1959) on February 12th 1910 on Saba. They had three children:

Sidney Clement, Carl Aubrey (who became a Major with the USAF) and Myrtice Carmen Leverock.

John George Hassell Leverock Jr. died in Barbados, BWI about 1963.

Thomas Charles Barnes

Thomas Charles Barnes, better known as TC, was born on Saba on July 2nd 1894, a son of Richard Thomas 'Buddy' Barnes (1860-xxxx) and Mary Ann Every (1862-xxxx). His siblings were Richard Thomas "Buddy" Jr., Chandlis Augustin, Araminta 'Minty', Estelle, Elizabeth Ethel and Robert Carlton Barnes. He married Elizabeth Nina Dowling, a daughter of Peter John Hassell Dowling (1864-1917) and Joanna Lovelace Hassell (1870-1964).

His father was a captain and owner of schooners, as well as his brothers Chandlis, Robert, Willie (lost at sea in a hurricane), and "Buddy Jr" who died at sea while Mate on a six-masted schooner.

TC was a maritime enterpriser; he 'cut his teeth' sailing the high seas with his seafaring family which provided him with a keen eye for good ships. He bought, owned, operated and sold several schooners such as 'Roma', 'Lillian', 'Nina' and the sloop "Carmen Maria", all of which frequently called on Saba. Although native from Saba, he lived part of his life in St Barths where, besides his regular shipping trade amongst the islands, he was an entrepreneur; he had a grocery and other import and export businesses. He acquired a considerable amount of land part of which later ended up in the hands of Mr. David Rockefeller. In his old age he was hard of hearing. Rumor has it that when Mr. Rockefeller asked to buy the property the captain asked for forty thousand dollars. Mr. Rockefeller said that he did not hear him thinking the price was too high. TC turned his good ear to him and said: "Son what did you say your name was?" The answer was "David Rockefeller". Mr. Barnes said: "Well since you did not hear me, let me tell you that the price of the land is Four Hundred Thousand Dollars." Mr. Rockefeller then asked Mr. Barnes, "Can I talk to you through the forty thousand dollar ear?" "I didn't hear you", replied Capt. Barnes, and the deal was closed. In all honesty, this proved to be a tall tale as sales documents provide the trace of the final purchase. The only truth is that Mr. Rockefeller did end up the piece of land.

On the land in "Grand Colombier" Capt. Barnes was also raising cattle. Every morning a rowing boat would bring the milk to Gustavia and was sold at his grocery store. He used the land to off-load cattle from Anguilla and other islands. Sometime shortly after they would become "French" cows and could be sold directly to Guadeloupe without importing tax. He was a smart business man to exploit the system as many others were doing, and this became a big industry in St-Barth and Saint Marteen.

He was also in the alcoholic-beverage industry as well. He operated a liquor trade business bottling several liquor products such as '*Red Cock*' and even distributed and bottled cask rum under the name '*Jack Iron*' from Grenada. The charred-oak cask rum was extremely strong and had to be diluted before bottling. As for "Red Cock" it is unclear what kind of product it was, since TC stopped with bottling of liquor before his son returned from Aruba after the closing of Lago Oil.

Charles Barnes was not one to forget where he came from and was also a kind man, always looking after the basic needs of his family and friends. In a letter addressed to TC, his cousin Jacob 'Jackie' Barnes thanked him for some clothes and food stuff he had received. "*It was some years I had never drink coffee from the seed. I blesses your dear kind hands each time I goes to eat a meal you sent me. Many thanks for the 3 pants I also received. They are a little long and a little big in the waist, but my daughter Alma is fixing them for me to wear.*"

It is said that behind extraordinary men there is usually an extraordinary woman. Everybody says Nina was a tough lady, a great business woman who ran the show while her husband was out at sea. And this is quite understandable as we analyze the information on her mother Joanna Lovelace Dowling (nee Hassell) who was a busy lady with her husband working in NYC, some of her children living in the United States, and from ship manifests we can trace her, even into old age, traveling very often between the island of St. Barths and NYC. It never ceases to amaze me how some people in those days took to the boats like a New Yorker to the subway.

After his wife died it was hard time for him in St. Barths; that is one of the reasons his son Charles Lovelace came back – of course, Lago was closing down too. His son was operating a business in Philipsburg, and they had a sloop to carry goods between the two islands (Dutch white potatoes, beer, etc.). TC Barnes died on Saint Barths on April 15, 1975.

Edmund Wilfred 'Will' Leverock

He was the fifth child born at the village of St. John's, Saba on December 7th 1888 to the family of John George Hassell Leverock Sr. (1852-1931) and Catherine Kelly Winfield (1863-1938).

He married Lillian Johnson, a daughter of Capt. Henry Hasselll Johnson (1852-1900) and Adeline Mardenborough (1857-1929); they had five children, namely: Catherine Wilma, Oscar, Allen, John and Carl Leverock.

He travelled to USA aboard the steamer Booth Line in 1914 and worked very hard on and off many ships and using as his local address our famous 27 South St. in New York, Mr. Kaliski's store. In between trips he found time to apply and obtain his naturalization which he obtained in December 3rd 1917 by the District Court of Boston, Mass. After five and a half years of laboring, he was ready to see his family and sent in a request for passport in 1919 to be able to travel and see them.

He enlisted for both World Wars (Jun 1917 and Jan 1945). He was the Third Mate of the SS Malacca, Second Mate aboard the SS Saxon (James Hassell was the Master) and the SS Audrey II.

He died on December 25th 1960 in Richmond Hill, New York.

Thomas Aubrey Leverock

Born on November 14th 1886 in the village of St. John's on Saba, he was one of the children of Capt. John George Hassell Leverock Sr. and Catherine Kelly Winfield.

As his brother, he was a Merchant Marine. He married Rosalina 'Lina' Johnson, a daughter of Peter James Johnson (1857-1904) and Elenor 'Ella' Every on Saba one January 17th 1917. They had three girls: Amy Marguerite, Audrey Hope and Evelyn Winifred.

Thomas Aubrey Leverock and his wife 'Lina' Johnson, would take his daughters Amy and Audrey, and his niece Estelle Simmons to spend quite some time on Barbados. Once, Estelle spent from May 20th, 1944 to March 9th, 1945 on Barbados. She had also spent time there in 1938.

We found this poem in her friend's book:

"Barbados Land of Happy dreams,
Amid Atlantic waves,
with Radiant sun and towering palms.
Blue skies and sunny seas.
And beaches white, and clean.
Dear Isle where I have spent happy months.
Oh ever dear to me. Sunshine or shade where'ere I be
I'll ever think of thee."

He introduced his declaration of intent and petition of naturalization in March 1916, which he obtained in the District Court of the City of New York, NY on September 5th 1916. The witnesses to his petition were Herman L. Every and Hyman Kaliski.

He enlisted for WW I in his capacity of seaman on July 29th 1918 and was discharged with a rank of Lieutenant on July 15, 1919; he also enlisted in WW II indicating his place of residence as 112-22 93rd Ave., Richmond Hill, NY.

He worked on the SS Pancras together with his young brother Bernard and his fellow countryman Edward Donalyene Hassell. He also was the Chief Mate of the Chinese vessel Yung Tsin from Honolulu to New York in 1946.

Thomas Aubrey Leverock and family with niece Estelle Simmons on Barbados

On September 1921 he is working with Thomas Hassell, both as Quartermasters aboard the SS Philadelphia which just came back from Curacao, DWI. In 1922 he was the Second-Mate of the SS Catherine with James C. Every (23) as an Able-Bodied Seaman[9]; the SS Haiti in 1922 where he was Second Mate. He also worked for the Colombia SteamShip Co as Third Mate aboard the SS Bolivar in 1925. By 1927 we find him working on the SS Haiti from St. Thomas and Cuba as First Officer. He as Mate of the SS Malabar in 1929. As he moves on to the Marine Transport Lines company (local agent for the US Maritime Commission) he works as Jr. Third Mate aboard the SS Glorieta which at age 59 could have been interpreted as a "demotion" but a smart move which put him on to longer routes to the US Naval Tanker "Tonti" and the SS Central

---

[9] Able-Bodied (AB) Seamen are mariners that serve as a ship's helmsmen, relying on visual references, sextants and compasses, and in large ships a rudder angle indicator, to steer a the course as directed by the mate or other officer on the bridge.

Victory where he was the Third Mate in 1946-1953, plying through Iceland, Morocco, Newfoundland and as far as Sasebo, Japan.

He was laid to rest on Dec 19 1977 in Pinellas, FL according to the *Department of Veterans Affairs BIRLS Death File.*

John William Leverock

He was the third son of John William 'Bo Willy" Leverock (1848-1937) and Ann Rebecca Crossley (1859-1929). His siblings were William Clark, Ethelbert, Hyacinth, Roland, Godfrey Carmel, Romilla, Leonede, Adelina and Oswin Cyrillus Leverock. He married Alice Hassell (1887-1949) a daughter of Henry Bloomfield Hassell (1849-1919) and Rose Ellen Holm (1852-1929).

He arrives to the USA in November 1898 aboard the ship Lizzie Berrell, and lives for 18 years in Providence, RI working as a carpenter.

He had already obtained US Citizenship at the US District Court of Providence, RI on February 25th 1911. About November 1917, he requested a passport for the purpose of bringing his wife and children to the states.

John William Leverock

He moved to New York and established residence at 1933 Greene Ave, Brooklyn NY. On May 7 1918, he arrived to USA with his wife Alice, and children John Harvey (8), Agnes Stella (5) and Joseph Leo (1). He moved to Washington Ave, Queens, NY before the 1920 Census was taken.

His youngest Helen Adeline was born in New York about 1920. He enlisted for both WW I & WW II; his father was part owner (3/8) of the schooner "Harbinger", co-owned by John Adolphus van Romondt from St. Maarten.

John William Leverock died at about 76 years of age in 1956.

James Cecil Every

Cecil was born on May 5th 1899 and was the fourth child of thirteen born from the union of Peter Anthony Every (1862-1941) and Laurentina Hassell. His siblings were: Aubrey Cleveland, Mabel, Reginald, Anna Sorina, Evelin, Olive, Mary, Sadie, Alma Louise, Alice Florence, Earl and the well know Alvin Lloyd 'Bobby' Every. He married Elsie Every, a daughter of Peter Anthony Every (1862-1941) and Laurentina Hassell

He arrived to New York for the first time in June 1919 aboard the SS Tennyson, traveling with his brother Aubrey, both visiting their uncle Henry Every. When Cecil retired he became an old farmer, however in his younger days he used to sail. He sailed to New Caledonia (belongs to France, next to Australia) to transport nickel for the USA. He sailed to many other places, including being on schooners which were wrecked on the reefs off the coast of Barbuda for insurance purpose. Not Cecil's decision of course, he was only a sailor.

He traveled and worked on several capacities aboard freighters such as: SS Catherine (Able Seaman), SS Mount Clay, Mount Caroll (Quartermaster); in 1930 he was on the payroll of Cuba Distilling Company out of Curtis Bay, MD working aboard the SS Cassimie as a Boatswain.

Lovelock Holm

Lovelock Holm with his first wife Ruth Evangeline Hunt

Lovelock Holm, 91, a veteran of World War I and chief engineer at Federal Paperboard for 43 years, died at the Meadows Convalescent Home in Manchester.

He was born April 22, 1887, in Saba, Dutch West Indies, the son of Mr. and Mrs. Thomas Holm. He was married in Norwich on September 21, 1920, to Helen L. Holm, who survived him.

Holm, a graduate of the Howley School of Engineering in Boston, Mass., served as master engineer in the U.S. Army and was machinist mate in the naval battalion. Serving on the executive committee as secretary-treasurer of the American Society of Mechanical Engineers, he organized the Norwich chapter of the engineering society.

Holm was active in the Boy Scouts and Junior Midshipmen Sea Scouts for many years, served on the Norwich Republican Town Committee, and was the second vice commander of Robert Fletcher Post 4, of Norwich

American Legion. Until his death he was the oldest living member of the Haverhill Merrimac Masonic Lodge in Haverhill, Mass.

Surviving besides his widow were one son, George Holm of Canterbury; two daughters, Ethel Paton of Pasadena, Cal., and Helen Virginia 'Ginny' Butterfield of Bolton; one sister Ida Irene Holm of Saba, Dutch West Indies; 13 grandchildren, several great grandchildren and great-great grandchildren, and several nieces and nephews."

Someone wrote below the announcement "Also a son, Roland of Cove Junction, Oregon."

Lovelock left Saba for the USA around 1907 to live but had been sailing on large schooners from there for a number of years already. He was one of seven siblings of the couple Thomas James Benjamin Holm (1850-1913) and Ann Catherine Hassell (1853 -1927). Lovelock was married twice. His first wife was Ruth Evangeline Hunt whose parents were from Derbyshire England by whom he had two children, Ethel Evelyn and Roland Henry Holm. His first wife died young and later he married Helen Little Corriguex and had two children by her, George B. Holm and Helen Virginia 'Ginny' Holm (1925-1998).

In his younger days, as so many of our Saba men back then, he sailed on a number of the old four master schooners. An article written in the Yankee of March 1963 prompted him to write a letter to the author. (I cannot find that particular Magazine issue on e-Bay. If anyone can get me a copy would appreciate it).

The letter is dated March 15, 1963 and is from Lovelock Holm living in Norwich, CT to Mr. Loren E. Haskell of Yankee Magazine in Dublin, New Hampshire.

"Dear Sir:

Your write-up in the YANKEE of March, 1963, "Ladies of the Sea", was a fine description of those beautiful ships. I, too, spent several years on the Palmer fleet.

I left the ocean in 1908. We took a load of coal to San Juan, Puerto Rico under Capt. Sumpter from Tennents Harbor, Maine. I was on the "Elizabeth Palmer" under Capt. Smith, of Norwood, Mass. He was a fine captain! I also was with Capt. Potter on the "Rebecca Palmer" which was built in Rockland, Maine. Capt. Potter was from Connecticut.

Most of my sailing was on the "Fred A. Davenport" with Capt. Freemont Kimball of Booth Bay Harbor. I am sure your dad used to know our captain. I remember the "Cora F. Cressy". She was a beautiful ship! Did you know Capt. Kimball, or Elery MacCauley, who was first mate? MacCauley's brother was steward on the "Fred A. Davenport". Was the "Cora F. Cressy" owned by the Winslow's from Portland, Maine.

I was also on the "Edith Folwell" under a captain from Connecticut.

Did you know a Mr. Steer from Deer Island? He was first mate with Capt. Sumner on the "Singleton Palmer". Did you know Capt. Tullock? I made a trip with him. I believe the ship's name was "Lizzie Borden." On board was the Borden girl who killed her step-mother. She was a beautiful girl and very polite. There was no mention in the trial of her taking the trip with Capt. Tulleck and his wife.

The Kimball's had a jewelry store in Bath, Maine. There were two children, a boy and a girl. The boy had a limp in one leg. They were wonderful folks. Check and see if you can remember some of the names which I have listed. We used to haul coal to the Maine central yard in Portland; also to the Bangor and Roosti terminal at Searsport, Maine, as well as, to the Mystic docks in Boston. I wonder how many of these brave men are still living. Is your father still living? Did you know the foreman of the sail loft at Portland? It was operated by the Winslow's. Many times I visited at their works for sails.

It was nice for you to write the article on those ships. Hoping to hear from you, I remain. Yours truly

Lovelock Holm

P.S. Did you know any Capt. Simmons* of New York; or Blakes from Pleasantville, N.J.? They were connected with the "Bull Line" from Baltimore Maryland. L.H.

*The Capt. Simmons referred to in the letter was Capt. Thomas Simmons of Saba who was a captain on several of the "Bull Line" ships. Also the "Rebecca Palmer" had at least one Saba captain which was Capt. Lockland Heyliger. Many men from Saba, sailed on this great five master.

Mr. Holm received a reply to his letter on March 22nd, 1963 from Mr. Haskell;

"Dear Sir,

I was delighted to receive your letter of the 15th, which was forwarded to me by YANKEE. Your letter was very interesting and you have quite a background in connection with the great schooners. You have sailed on some fine vessels.

As you suggested I have checked some of the names you mentioned in your letter and I certainly do remember them. Such as, Capt. Dan Smith of the "Elizabeth Palmer", and Capt. Dave Sumner of the "Rebecca Palmer". Also, Capt. William Totter of the "Singleton Palmer". I realize of course that these captains changed around and were on different vessels as you and I came in contact with them I have heard my father mention the name of Captain Freemont Kimball of Boothbay Harbor, when he was captain of the "Fred A. Davenport". My father was captain of the "Alice May Davenport" at one time or another. Yes I recall making trips to those ports you mentioned. Yes the "Sara Cressy" was owned by the J.S. Winslow's of Portland at one time. She was originally owned by Percy and Small of Bath, Maine. My father was a large owner during her early career. She went under in 1917. He had taken the five-masted "Mary W. Bowen" to Buenos Aires, Argentina with a load of coal and on the return passage north to New York a cargo of quebracho wood, which is used for medicinal purposes. He was 60 years old at the time and it was a hazardous trip and he was a sick man and died about two months later in a hospital in Boston.

You must have had many anxious moments in various storms at sea. There were the hurricane, snow storms, and fog to contend with. I guess we are both luck to be alive today. My last trip was with my father on the 5 master "Governor Brooks" in 1913. I do not think there are many of us left today. One had to be courageous, skillful, and daring, and reliable.

I thank you again for your splendid letter. We may run across each other some way in the future. We would have a lot to talk about. Write again when you have time. Cordially Yours.

Loren E. Haskell.

P.S. Yes I remember the sail loft of Winslow's at Portland, and their ship chandler's store."

Lovelock Holm also had a brother Benjamin who was a chemist of note in the United States as well. The correspondence between these two gentlemen confirm much of what we have written about Sabans working on large four and five master schooners of the Palmer fleet and many other lovely four master schooners built in Bath Maine, Gloucester, Mass., and Nova Scotia.

Lovelock lived an interesting life and never forgot Saba. Will Johnson has somewhere in his library some other interesting documents relating to him but could not put his hand on them to contribute to this article. May his memory be blessed.

Carl Hassell

Another brother of Capt. Abraham, Carl Hassell a merchant, has a long interview in Dr. Julia Crane's book "Saba Silhouettes" where he makes comments on the entire family including Capt. Abe who used to buy schooners in New England and Nova Scotia and resell them to Sabans living here as well as on Barbados.

Carl Hassell and his second wife Maud Hassell

Carl was born on September 25th 1886, the ninth child of William James Benjamin Hassell (1840-1924) and Elizabeth Hassell (1843-1924). He married Madge Hassell (1888-1917), the eldest daughter of Henry Johnson Hassell (1844-1921) and Ann Elizabeth Every, on Jan 3rd, 1912 and had two daughters: Elaine and Lena Louise.

He was a naturalized US citizen and enlisted during WW I. After his first wife died in Providence, RI he went back to Saba. He finally re-married on June 30th 1937.

He died December 13th 1973 on Saba.

James Anthony Simmons

In 1984 Will Johnson interviewed James Anthony Simmons. He was still alive and active in 2009 when he reached to be 95 years of age this year.

He was born on Saba on August 9th, 1914. His mother was Caroline Maria Simmons born Every who died around 1956. Her parents were Mamselle Every, also known as "Zellie," whose people originally came to Saba from St. Thomas, and her husband was named Peter Every.

James Anthony Simmons and Saba Historian Will Johnson

James Anthony's father was named James Arthur Simmons and he died around 1943 in Barbados at the age of 55. His parents were Sally Jones and Alexander Simmons. They were all dead before James Anthony was born.

His father James Arthur Simmons had left Saba and went to live in Barbados to work for "Redhead" Joe Simmons who had moved from Saba as many Sabans had done at the time. Redhead Joe used to own Walmar Lodge which was a plantation at the time.

James Anthony had not known his father and, as so many young boys at the time, he decided to go to sea and the usual age in those days was 14. And so at that young age James Anthony went to work as a mess boy on the schooner the *"Ina Vanterpool"*. It was a large schooner measuring 105 feet long, 26 feet wide and 218.90 tons. This two-masted schooner belonged to Captain Tommy Vanterpool. The Captain was Herman Simmons. They sailed between Curacao and the Windward Islands with the mail. The schooner had no motor and a trip, depending on weather conditions going and coming would take as much as ten days each way. Going down to Curacao would be faster and would usually take three to four days, but coming back could be from ten to twelve days. He also sailed on the "Georgetown" a schooner which was 81 feet long, 26 feet wide and 118.72 tons.

This schooner would carry as many as 75 passengers who had to rough it out on deck mostly. They made a monthly trip to Curacao and in between would sail usually between Saba and St. Kitts. Around 1929 or 1930 the "Georgetown" went ashore on the island of Nevis and got destroyed there. James Anthony was not on board at the time, though I had an Uncle Herbert Simmons who was just a young boy himself who went ashore with her. In those days it took several weeks before my grandparents knew that he was safe and sound. James Anthony also worked on the "Three Sisters" with Capt. Will Leverock.

After that James Anthony sailed on the "Rhode Island" a two-masted which sailed to Curacao and which replaced the "Three Sisters." She also belonged to Captain William Benjamin Hassell. Her master at the time was Capt. Aldrick Dowling. She was destroyed in a hurricane in Frederiksted, St. Croix around 1929. James Anthony and the crew had come to St. Thomas from Curacao. They went south to run from the hurricane and struck a reef just off the harbor of Frederiksted. Fortunately, no lives were lost. When daylight cleared the pilot boat came out and took the passengers and crew ashore. They were unable to save the boat but most of the supplies were saved. Mr. Labega (a son of Freddie Labega of St. Maarten) who was married to a red-haired girl from Saba and who lived there put them all up at his home. There were about twenty passengers on board when the accident happened. The two-masted schooner "Mary C. Santos" also belonging to Capt. Ben Hassell then came up from Barbados to St. Croix to pick them up. The passengers were all from the surrounding islands.

After that he went to work on the two-masted schooner the "Francis W. Smith" a salt fish runner from Canada which belonged to Captain Johnny Vanterpool and them.

The Captain was Aldrick Dowling. These schooners were all built in Canada. They would bring in codfish and lumber to Barbados and the Sabans would buy them there. On the "Francis W. Smith" he was an ordinary seaman and sailed to Trinidad, Demerara, Martinique and Guadeloupe carrying gasoline in drums from Trinidad. He did this for three years. The schooner was sold and then the captain went fishing off the coast of Guyana.

Around 1935 he went to Curacao where he worked for "Pletterij Nederhorst," and then on to Aruba where he joined the "Mosquito" fleet. This was a fleet of tankers which belonged to ESSO on which a number of Sabans lost their lives in World War II.

Many of the survivors who worked 15, 20 and more years and who then still lived on Saba got a big fat pension of fls.20.- and less per month (Yes, That much) for having risked their lives before during and after the war for ESSO on Aruba. James Anthony worked for about twenty years on the fleet. He mostly sailed between Aruba and Lake Maracaibo, but sometimes to Barbados, Brazil and to Mobile, Alabama and Norfolk, Virginia and to the port of Colon in Panama.

In 1945 he married Aline Hughes from which marriage three children were born. After he came back to Saba he sailed with Capt. Randolph Dunkin on the sloop the "Eden Rock", mostly between Saba and St. Kitts. Most of the trade was with St. Kitts back then. The last time he sailed on a regular basis was in the sixties on the sloop "Santa Lou" also belonging to Capt. Dunkin and which carried the mail between Saba and Sint Maarten, when Saba had an empty airport and they said no plane could land here.

James Anthony was also active in the politics since the sixties and was on the WIPM list each election since 1971 with Peter Granger and Will Johnson.

He was a joiner, but not the carpenter/ship-builder type, but a social one. When Miss Carmen and others started the Women's Organization he joined. When asked why he had joined he said, "Them poor women need help." If the Women's Organization still exists I am sure that he is still a member in good standing.

James Anthony had been one of the main servers in the Roman Catholic Church in The Bottom. He had been a pillar of his church and was a member of the Parish council and was also a Member of the Living Water Community.

For many years he was also a housepainter by profession. Once when he was painting Will Johnson's roof, his son Teddy who was a little boy back then used to think that he was "Santa Claus" because it was around Christmas time and he had learned that Santa always landed on the roof. And since old James Anthony was on the roof for a couple of days, Teddy thought that he was Santa.

When he could get around he was always to be found to help out with all kinds of social activities and was a real asset to the people of The Bottom in particular and the people of Saba in general. He retired from the sea when he was in his eighties but still enjoyed fishing, especially with his friend Elmer Linzey. He always had fond memories of a life spent at sea. Especially the years he spent on the old Saban owned schooners trading throughout the West Indies

And as it's often the case in small island communities such as Saba's, many also had a family relationship. As a boy Will Johnson remembers a big tall brown man stopping him and asking if he was Johnson's boy and he said: "Yes." He said to Will "You know, me and you are family!"

"You bet," Will thought to himself. "How can you be family to me?" Anyway when Will got home he asked his mother and described the man to her. She laughed and said: "That must be Long Charlie. Yes he and your father are first cousins." Turns out Will's great uncle Henry Johnson was his father. "Long Charlie" was Charles and a brother of our friend James Anthony.

James Anthony attended every event he could make it to, and was fully alert as to what was going on around him. He would have been 95 in 2009. Will Johnson made a speech for him at his 90th birthday and it seems like yesterday. Until his last days, he lived at home and was surrounded by his grandchildren and great grandchildren and it was always a pleasure to see how they appreciated having him around.

He died on Saba on May 4th 2004.

Herbert Rexford Every

Herbert Rexford Every was the sixth son of James Every (1864-1926) and Millicent 'Millie' Hassell, born in Saint John's, Saba on July 25, 1901. His siblings were Cattey May, Aramintha, Daisy, James Dudley, James MacDonald, Abraham Thomas and Ivan Isaac.

He was the master of the British Schooner "Florence M. Douglas" owned by Peter S. Hassell who, as many other Sabans of the time, was living at St. Michael, Barbados.

On May 4th, 1942 the German U-Boat (U-162) was very active operating off the coast of British Guiana sinking American SS Eastern Sword at 9:43 AM, 12 miles North of Georgetown. The Schooner "Florence M. Douglas" a three-masted schooner, unescorted and unarmed was trading the route from Bonaire, Netherlands Antilles to Georgetown, British Guiana and 40 miles northeast of Anna Regina. At 7:00 PM was she intercepted by the U-Boat who made them stop with a shot across her bow. The Germans shouted their orders the crew instructing them to abandon ship immediately. As the men attempted to collect their personal belongings instead of leaving the ship as ordered, the U-Boat shot two more warning rounds and restated their orders. The crew of the schooner boarded immediately their lifeboat and separated from the doomed ship, rowing southbound toward the coast. After the men where in the clear, the U-boat captain Jürgen Wattenberg ordered to blow the schooner out of the water from a distance of about 200 yards; they fired 18 rounds from their 88mm deck gun, shooting away the rigging and halyards, cutting down the topmasts and destroying the superstructure until the schooner sank with a final fatal-blow along the waterline. The schooner went down about 65 miles of the Georgetown Beacon. As the crew rowed the lifeboat in a southerly direction an aircraft approached the scene, but the U-boat evaded an attack by crash diving. The survivors later made landfall at Anna Regina and were then transported to Georgetown, where they arrived on May 7.

Herbert Rexford Every was married to Ruby Dowling on September 15th 1926 on Saba. She was the youngest daughter of John William Dowling (1865-1936) and Mary Elizabeth Hassell (1872-1909).

Dedric Ambrose Every

He was the third son of John Leverock Every (1861-1939) and Bernardina Elizabeth 'Deena' Hassell (1873-1964), born on Saba on Jan 9th 1902. He married Marie Magdalena Burton from South Boston on March 26th 1926 and they had one son, Reverend Dedric Clarence Every.

He came to the USA via Curacao aboard the SS Philadelphia on March 28, 1920. He became a US Citizen registered at the District Court of Maryland, Baltimore Dec 2nd 1924 and lived at 734 S. Decker Ave., Baltimore, MD.

He was a seaman aboard the SS Edith and the SS Muskogee, however he decided not to go back to sea and worked as an electrician. He died on November 5th, 1999 in Glenn Arm, Baltimore, MD.

Peter Every

On an island where nine tenths of the men at one time or another had been mariners, many are the tales Will Johnson heard in his youth of our schooners and adventures at sea. Mr. Peter Every, one of our former seamen who resided in Windwardside, recounted for the Saba Herald two adventures at sea in which he was involved.

The first episode took place in 1921. He could not remember the exact date, but during the year in question he was sailing on the two-masted schooner 'Margie Turner'. At that time the vessel was under the command of David Hassell, and Clifford Johnson.

Peter stated that the 'Margie Turner' left Saba bound for Curacao under a fair breeze all the way. It was about forty-eight hours after their departure one afternoon that Captain David took a longitude sight and told them that towards midnight they would see the lighthouse in Bonaire. Exactly when eight bells were striking there was a thunderous crash and the 'Margie Turner' was ashore on a reef sixty miles to the east of Bonaire (A sailor, who was striking the bell at the time of the incident, went headfirst down below to the cabin).

The Captain immediately ordered the lifeboat over the side, and the crew headed for what turned out to be a barren reef about thirty miles long. There was neither water nor food on the place.

The following day the Captain, the mate and the cook left with the lifeboat and started to row for the island of Bonaire, sixty miles away.

As the dawn of each succeeding day broke over the heads of those left behind, their hunger and thirst became unbearable. They drank sea water, which merely increased their thirst, and the only things they could find to eat were the raw whelks they picked from the reef.

One day they saw a schooner passing very close, and they tied a piece of cloth to a stick to attract attention. But the schooner did not stop. Later it was learned that it was Captain Lawrence Johnson from Saba, on his way from Curacao to Barbados.

After seven horrible days on the reef, a fishing boat from the island of Bonaire came to their rescue when the disaster had been reported by the Captain. The fishing boat then took them to Curacao.

Peter Every lived to experience yet another tragedy, which happened during World War II. Here follows his story as related for the Saba Herald.

It was a sunny yet windy Saturday in mid-April 1943, when the ship I was sailing on eased out from the oil docks of the Esso refinery at Aruba, bound for Panama in the Canal Zone. Our ship 'SS Valera', one of the lake tanker fleet that plied between Lake Maracaibo and Aruba, was deeply loaded with heavy fuel oil. The skipper, Captain Russell, and the other officers were British while the other crew members were from the Dutch Antilles. Also on board was a Norwegian sailor as passenger. The next day, Sunday, the weather worsened and our ship began taking waves over the bows. Sunday night at eight bells (midnight), I went to the bridge to relieve the quartermaster at the wheel, who was also a Saban named Walter Woods. Shortly after Woods left to go aft, where the crew's sleeping quarters were located, there was a sudden thunderous explosion. The ship felt as if she had been lifted out of the sea by a tremendous force while the men on the bridge were flung to the deck.

We all knew at that moment that we had been torpedoed. The tanker 'Valera' now lay dead on the water, and took a heavy list to port as oil from her ruptured tanks poured overboard. Captain Russell ordered the life rafts thrown overboard and to abandon ship. There was the sound of tortured metal as the ship, her back broken, parted in two. As the two halves drifted apart, we could see the men in the stern section lowering the lifeboats. The Captain and I were the last two left on the bridge, the others having taken to the rafts, which were still alongside. The Captain ordered me to the raft, saying: "The Captain is the last to leave." I tried to persuade him to come with me, but he refused to do so. The bow section of the ship was now so much listed, that it was necessary for me to climb down a pipe in order to gain the deck which at times was buried under water. I clung to the rail, waiting for a chance to jump to the raft, when I heard the Captain yell: "Look out Every!" Thinking it was something about to fall on me from aloft, I glanced up. At the same time I felt a terrific blow against my thigh, my hands were torn away from the rail, and I was flung overboard, landing asprawl on the raft. The men on the raft, realizing that I was injured tried to make me as comfortable as possible. Captain Russell was now clinging to the wing of the bridge and was in danger of falling. We called to him to jump. Unfortunately, when he did, he fell in the oil that was still pouring out of the ship. He went under and never surfaced again. There were now five of us on the raft: the first and second mates, the chief steward, the Norwegian sailor and myself. The bow section of the 'Valera' sank shortly afterward, but we could see the stern section still afloat in the distance. Just after daybreak, a huge wave struck the raft, washing me overboard. I surfaced partly under the raft and might have drowned. Luckily the Norwegian sailor saw me. He hauled me out and lifted me back on the raft. I am very thankful to that young giant who saved my life.

About midday a huge hammerhead shark bore down on the raft. For a moment it seemed that he was actually going to attack us on the raft, but at the last moment he dived under us. For hours afterward the monster circled the raft, while we watched and held on to ropes, in terror of being washed overboard to be eaten by the creature. Suddenly the shark changed direction and headed for the raft and again dived underneath us, but this time he got stuck when halfway underneath. Our raft began to shake and heave, as the beast struggled frenziedly to free himself. For hours this continued, until eventually his movements lessened and then ceased entirely. Our raft now had a man-eating shark as passenger down there.

On the morning of the second day, the stern end of the ship disappeared, and neither raft nor life boats could be seen. The first mate rationed the food and water, saying it might be days or weeks before we could be rescued. Then on Saturday morning, seven days after our ship was sunk, a Catalina flying boat appeared, circled around us and dropped a flare, indicating that help was on the way. Sure enough, three hours later an American cruiser came up with a bone in her teeth and stopped near us. A landing net was put over the side, by which means our men climbed on board with the assistance of the sailors. Because my hip was broken I had to be taken on board on a stretcher. One of the warship's officers asked: 'what is that thing under your raft?' The first mate replied: 'That thing is a hammerhead shark that has scared the hell out of us.' A couple of minutes later there was a sound of rapid gunfire and shark and raft were chopped in pieces.

I was taken to Panama, where I was hospitalized for six months, and then sent on to Aruba, where I learned that two others of our crew had suffered broken bones. Our Captain, a fine man and a good seaman, was the only casualty.

William James 'Jamesie' Linzey

Jamesie was one out of ten children born to James Linzey (1871-1917) and Edilca Heyliger (1877-1913). His siblings were Wilfred, Alexander, Joseph Evan, Nellie Francis, Clinton, Muriel 'Moo', Theodore, John Alvin and Faith Eulalie.

He was tooted by many old timers as one "the best fisherman of the past"; he built his reputation over time, starting at a very young age when he would skip school once every week, grab his favorite pole and head to the rocks. As he grew older he felt the need to work for himself, especially after his father died. With his uncle and his oldest brother they would take the fishing traps of his father and learn the business of commercial fishing.

As many Sabans of the day, Jamesie also had to learn planting, raising livestock he received from his father and also do some hunting.

His seafaring skills were developed by the many seasoned people like Randolph Dunkin who used him as a hand on his sloop "Nautilius". In December 1934 he was sailing with Dunkin taking cargo; that evening a strong gust of wind announcing a heavy storm made the ship capsize.

Suddenly Dunkin and his men, Garnet, Hilton Whitfield and Jamesie found themselves in the water.

Phyllis Randolph Dunkin

Captain Randolph Dunkin, known to all his friends as 'Rannie', was born on Saba on December 27th, 1907. His mother was Mary Dunkin from Below-The-Gap. He was born in old Capt. Will Simmons' home, which coincidentally now belongs to his nephew former Lt. Governor Wycliffe Smith.

Randolph's father was Captain Ernest Vanterpool, a member of the family which produced several captains and owners of schooners. Randolph went to school in the building where the Housing Foundation is now located.

His teachers were Sister Euphresine and Sister Georgine. Randolph also had four sisters on his mother's side of the family. One of those sisters was the well-known Mrs. Ruth Smith a great Christian, volunteer social worker and so on.

He started sailing in 1923. He left here with "Gardy" Hassell on the "Cyril" a 60 tons schooner which belonged to Mr W. H. Netherwood of St. Maarten. This schooner was lost on a reef, after a hurricane season, coming out of the Oyster Pond.

He then started sailing on the schooner the 'Virginia'. This schooner was owned by Captain Abraham Mardenborough and later sold to the government with Captain Abraham still in command. Captain Abraham was married to Miss Ohnie Wathey and they had a lovely old time mansion on the Front Street in St. Maarten. It was located on the beach across the street from the 'Oranje School'.

Later on Randolph went to sail on the "Ina Vanterpool' a large three master schooner which belonged to his uncle Captain Thomas Charles Vanterpool. After that he went to sail on the 'Thelma' a schooner owned by Captain Aldrick Dowling of St. John's. That schooner used to trade with Barbados and St. Thomas but also went to other places in the Caribbean. He later sailed on the large schooner the "Three Sisters" owned by Captain William Benjamin Hassell and his brothers.

When he started sailing he started out as a cabin boy and went to the islands around Saba like St. Kitts and St. Thomas. He went to Barbados on a trip with Capt. Will Leverock on the "Three Sisters" to put her on dry-dock and remained there for 15 days. They left here on a Monday and arrived there on a Friday morning. All the boats mentioned so far were strictly sailboats.

The motors only came with the large 145 foot schooner the "Mayflower" in 1929. This vessel was a large 2 master and belonged to Captain Thomas Charles Vanterpool. Her captain was Reuben Simmons of Hell's Gate. The schooner broke her bowsprit and both masts in 1931, to the North-East of Bonaire. She went to Bonaire, towed there by the Dutch Man-O-War the "B.K." There she underwent the necessary repairs and then sailed to Curacao. Captain Tommy sold her to someone in Jamaica and that's the last anyone heard of her. The "Thelma" went ashore in Tortola in the thirties. The "Virginia" in the gale of 1928, broke her moorage and was never heard of again. She was anchored in St. Kitts and did not have anyone on board. Captain Mardenborough was not on that trip.

Captain Conrad Richardson was captain at the time. Randolph used to sail once a month to Curacao with the "Ina Vanterpool" and the "Three Sisters". The "Mayflower" made the trip every two weeks. He sailed with Capt. T. C. Vanterpool and Capt. Reuben Simmons mostly. Captain Reuben was not there the time she broke her masts, Luke Vlaun was the captain.

Later on he went to Curacao to work for the SHELL oil company, on boats bringing crude oil from Lake Maracaibo in Venezuela. This he did for about one year. Then he went to Aruba where he worked for ESSO for two years on Lago's oil fleet. He came back home to Saba in 1939.

Before that time, in 1932, he owned a sloop named the "Nautilus" which he bought from Granville van Romondt for fls.1.250. She got lost between St. Kitts and Statia in 1934. The wind just came up strong and rolled her over. They had a flat bottom 9 ft boat on board. He and his brother Garnet Hughes rowed into Statia to get help. They left William James Linzey and Hilton Whitfield on the upturned wreck. This accident happened at 10:30 pm, they arrived in Statia at 1:00 am at the Police Station. They picked up two boats and accompanied by police officer Van Zanten they headed back to the wreck. They had lights with them. Randolph was in one boat and Garnet in the other. Hilton saw the light and gave a whoop. According to Captain Randolph, Hilton and Jamesy looked like two wet rats. They got back safely into Statia on a Saturday morning.

In 1939 on his return to Saba he bought the "*Energy*" a "cobalt" Tortola boat, one mast. He bought it from J. A. W. Georges, a Tortola merchant for US $300.—He had that sloop until the war was declared and then he sold her to the government for fls.900.--. He then went back to Aruba and worked there until he returned to Saba in 1946.

He bought another "cobalt style" vessel named the "Eden" in 1946 from Edward Tutt in Tortola. He paid U.S. $1.300.—for her and owned her until 1959, and then he bought the much larger "*Santa Lou*" from Blanche Potter in Tortola for US $ 4.600.—

Capt. Randolph was also shipwrecked on the sloop the "Bertha Johnson" which belonged to the Magras family on St. Barths. He went to St. Kitts and loaded with 120 sheets of asbestos for St. Barths. He left the "Eden" in St. Barths and took the "Bertha Johnson" and was on his second trip to St. Kitts when he got lost. The sloop had been built by Stanley Johnson in Sint Eustatius. This accident happened on the night of June 21st, 1949. All of his crew was lost. They were William Wilson, married to Rosalie Wilson, they had 7 or 8 children. Peter Linzey, brother of Maude Linzey. He was married to Christine a sister of Capt. Randolph's, and they lived at The Gap, and Desmond Levenstone, a bachelor. William Wilson and Peter Linzey were the grandfathers of former State Secretary Mrs. Amelia Nicholson, born Linzey.

Only Randolph survived. According to him it was a squally night, and then suddenly a thick squall loomed up out of nowhere. He decided to put in at Sandy Point. While going in, rain came in to the land. He put the helm into the wind, and she turned right over, about one and a half miles from the shore and within 2 or 3 minutes she sank. Desmond, Peter and Page got out from between the rigging. Randolph and Page were swimming on oars. He called out to the others. They continued to swim and call out to one another. After a while Desmond and the others did not respond. Page was fully clothed, and then all at once he said he couldn't hold out any longer, and just took in water like a bottle and sank away to his death in the depths.

After a while Randolph's foot touched the sand. He continued swimming in the dark until he felt his belly touch the sand. He had landed around Belle Tape Point, North of Sandy Point. He started swimming from around 10:30 pm and arrived at the Police station at 1 am. He walked along the beach and into Sandy Point by the bakery in front of the Police station. Right away Sergeant Bridgewater called on the telephone to town, but not until the next day at 10 am did the police boat leave Basseterre to look for survivors, but nobody was found. The police sent a cable to Saba to inform the families.

I was only a boy then, but I can still recall how upset people were over this calamity. Then people here had compassion for one another, more so than today. Randolph sold the "Eden" to Capt. Thomas Charles Barnes (aka TC) who lived in St. Barths for US $2.000.—plus he got $1.000.- to buy the motor for the "*Santa Lou.*" He owned the "*Santa Lou*" from 1959 to 1966, and then lost her in Anguilla. She was a total loss. This happened on the 2nd day of January 1966. James Anthony Simmons was with him. She brought up to shore with engine, sail and everything. This happened in the night and as the beach was so white it was difficult to estimate the distance to shore. The vessel was a total loss and he had no insurance.

He then bought the '*Roselle*' another sloop in Dominica from MacLawrence. He paid $13.500.—BWI for her. In 1973 he sold her to Max Nicholson who later sold her in the Virgin Islands.

Randolph's main run used to be between Saba and St. Kitts, but he made three trips to Puerto Rico for cement, 500 bags a trip which took all of 8 to 9 days in going and coming. He was a banker, a mailman, and used to withdraw money from the banks for people here and make deposits as well. Sabans then used to bank their money with the Royal Bank of Canada and Barclays Bank on St. Kitts. Saba merchants used to deal with John Gumbs (married to three Leverock sisters from Saba. Yes all three, not together, but in some form of succession.), Sahelie and other general merchants such as S.E.L. Horsford and company which was a lumber company.

One of the boats built on Saba which Randolph remembers was the '*Augusta*' built here by Horton and registered in Tortola. He also remembers making a trip on the '*Georgetown*' a two-masted Canadian built schooner around 60 to 70 tons which belonged to T. C. Vanterpool. She was first named the '*Olympic*' and belonged to Capt. Lovelock Hassell who had moved to Barbados. She went ashore in Nevis in 1928, the Captain was Herman Simmons who had moved to St. Maarten and lived on the Front Street. The '*Alice*' belonged to Hilvere Lawrence of Grand Case St. Maarten. She was a two-masted schooner and was rented by the Vanterpool's. She made several trips to Curacao but was not big enough for the trade. Then Captain Tommy went to Maine to buy the '*Mayflower*'.

Will Johnson did this interview back in 1984 and he wrote: "Captain Randolph still likes to sail and he goes up and down with Al and Eddie Hassell on their cargo boat the 'Brianne C.' I recently made a trip with them to Sint Eustatius to attend the funeral of Mr. Vincent Astor Lopes. Randolph was in the Captain's Chair and at 76 he is still quite active."

During his many years as Captain between Saba and St. Kitts he proved to be of great service to our people here on Saba. In 1976 he was decorated by H.M. the Queen for his outstanding services. A small isolated place like ours needs heroes of our own that our young people can look up to. Randolph, in our opinion, is a hero worth looking up to.

His son Willis passed away on Curacao. His daughter Paulette is alive and has lived all her life on Sint Eustatius. He has a number of grandchildren and great grandchildren on Statia. One of his grandsons was former Commissioner Neuman Pompier. He also had a niece Mrs. Marie Senior-Hughes living in Windwardside and of course his nieces Shirley and Yvonne Smith as well as Act. Lt. Governor Roy Smith, all living on Saba.

Randolph was married to Ms. Ursula Dunkin for whom the former Anglican Kindergarten was named. The street leading past his former home in The Bottom is named in his honor. I remember once some folks coming down from the USA looking up their family tree. One of the grandsons of Estelle Simmons-Vanterpool told Will Johnson that his grandmother, who lived in St. Thomas, told him that if any brown skinned people claimed to be an uncle or aunt to listen to them as her father had roamed around the town quite a bit. Some days later I passed the young man on a wall sitting with Randolph with a tape recorder interviewing him. Just a few months ago the same person was back on Saba and telling me stories he had heard from his' uncle Randolph'. Many of the people whom Captain Randolph used to help are all gone now but they always talked highly of him in appreciation of his many years of dedicated service. It would be difficult to image nowadays any number of merchants from especially the Windwardside giving Randolph money to deposit in their bank accounts on St. Kitts where he also had authority to withdraw monies from their accounts and pay bills on their behalf. It was another world back then and that is not so long ago when you come to think of it. Saba remembers you Captain 'Rannie' and pridefully so.

John Esmond Mathew Levenston

Captain John Esmond Mathew Levenston was born "Below-the-Gap" on Saba on October 3rd, 1912. He was the son of Joshua Levenston and Mrs. Emilia Levenston (nee Hassell). He married Hilda Claudine Sorton (1909-

1986), a daughter of Julitette Sorton. They had four children: Ishmael Matthew Ameal, Letchio Marie 'Lettie', Gloria 'Gee Gee' and Esmond Oliver Agustin Levenston. He passed away on St. Maarten on June 30, but was laid to rest on Saba on July 4th, 1994.

The world which he grew up in was much different to the Saba the young people know today. As many Sabans of previous generations, he did not have the privilege of attending school of any kind. In those days life was hard, and all family members had to do their part in order to survive. Yet as Matthews's life proved, his lack of a formal education did not serve as an impediment. A good dose of common sense and a willingness to work instilled by his parents led him forward to achieve much for Saba and its people.

As a mariner, he started sailing when he was eighteen with Captain Randolph Dunkin on a small sloop called the "Nautilus". His very first trip from St. Maarten on this ship nearly ended up in disaster as a windstorm caught the sloop just outside Fort Amsterdam and nearly turned her over. He continued sailing on that sloop for over a year. As was the custom back then, he, like many others headed for Curacao where he went to work for the Shell Oil Company. He started sailing on Shell oil tankers, one of which was name the "Alicia" which mostly sailed between Curacao and Lake Maracaibo hauling crude oil for the refinery.

After a couple of years he went to Aruba and worked there on Esso oil tankers, again hauling crude oil from Venezuela and carrying oil products between Aruba and Jacksonville Florida as well as to other ports along the Gulf of Mexico.

Sailing on an oil tanker during World War II was a very dangerous business as they were the targets of the German submarines known as U-boats which wanted to deprive the Allied Forces of much needed fuel of which two thirds were provided by the large oil refineries on Aruba and Curacao.

During World War II the tanker on which Mathew sailed came into the harbor in San Nicolas loaded down with crude oil for the Esso oil refinery. The tanker had to wait out in the harbor to get into berth as there were other tankers waiting as well. Little did they know that a German submarine was lurking below waiting to blow up the oil refinery. The submarine attacked during the night of February 16th, 1942, and Mathew and several Sabans had to take to the water in a sea of fire. The late Hubert Smith and Willa Every were also part of the crew of the tankers which went down, and they survived. Several other Sabans though lost their lives that night, while Mathew swam for eight hours. He swam from San Nicolas harbor all the way down to above the Strand Hotel in Oranjestad before he was picked up. The four tankers which were torpedoed were the "Pedernales", the "Oranjestad", the "Tia Juana" and the "San Nicolas." The "Pedernales" was beached and later restored. The tankers had a crew of 102 of which 47 lost their lives. Those from Saba were: Clifford Achilles Wilson Fireman, age 30, Kenneth Darcey Lynch, sailor 33, Eric Norbert Linzey, messboy 21, Anthony D. Jackson, student fireman age 37 and James Stewart Cornett, sailor age 28. They all sailed on the SS "Pedernales". On the SS "Tia Juana" John William Dunlock, Quartermaster born Saba Feb. 3, 1905 and Walter Whitfield born Saba August 12, 1912, Fireman also lost their lives. So on that one night alone Saba lost seven men in the attack on the Lago oil refinery. After that experience Mathew came back to Saba and he bought a small sloop called the "Astria" which he renamed the "Gloria" after his daughter. In the meantime he was married to Mrs. Hilda Levenston born Sorton, and together they had a total of eight children.

Captain Mathew and his rival Will Johnson survived many political storms on land, and together they also survived one at sea. The latter storm took place on September 1st, 1959. They left Saba at five in the evening, heading for St. Maarten. The other passenger was Mr. Percy Labega the father of Mr. Clem Labega among others.

Around eleven o'clock that night a sudden storm came up and there they were out in the middle of the ocean. Before they had left Saba, Captain Mathew had said that he did not like to leave as his uncle Fernandus (Feredoom) Hassell was dying and would call him back. Well call him back he certainly did. We passed through a night of sheer terror. By the next afternoon we had been tossed about and drifted till we ended up to the South of Saba. An oil tanker almost ran us over. It passed so close to the sloop that you could nearly touch its sides. Luckily the next day people spotted the crippled sloop drifting in the distance and a motor launch of Kenneth Peterson's came out and helped to tow us back into the roadstead in the late afternoon. In W.F.M. Lampe's book "Buiten de Schaduw van de Gouverneur" he has a chapter on how he, the then Minister of Finance Juancho Irausquin, and Lampe's daughter Sheila nearly got lost on the "Gloria" in a storm with Capt. Mathew. Lampe claims that Irausquin swore that if he survived that he would try and get some money from Holland to build an airport on Saba.

Other sloops which Mathew owned were the cobalt named the "Anna Louise" which went ashore in a hurricane on St. Maarten. Then he had the "Island Pride" which ran into the Diamond Rock by Saba and sunk. Once again Mathew found himself for five hours in the water. After that he bought the large sloop the "Fidelity B." On a trip to Statia the rudder of the sloop broke and it started to drift. He managed to anchor on the Saba Bank where he remained for four days. On the evening of the fourth day his anchor chain broke and the sloop went adrift once more. Leo Chance was Minister then and he gave the Dutch Marines directions on how to fly from Curacao. By that time Mathew had been listening on the radio as to how the search for him had been abandoned. But the Marine plane located him and threw out flares. A fruit boat rescued him about 150 miles South of Saba and took the sloop in tow, but it was later abandoned. Mathew and his son and the other crew members were taken with the fruit boat all the way to Panama from where they were able to fly back home. It was after that incident that Capt. Mathew decided to throw in the towel as far as sea life was concerned.

In the meantime Mathew had been a captain on land as well, and had quite a successful political career behind him. He ran for political office in 1951 and together with Mr. Ulric Hassell he became one of the Islands first Commissioners and he served on the Island Council as well. In that election Mathew only had 12 votes. The large vote getters were people like Kenneth Peterson, David Doncker, and Herman Hassell and so on. However the salary of Commissioner was fls. 50.—per month back then and the others were told that they could not own a business and be a Commissioner. By 1955 Mathew had proven himself and in turn became the biggest vote getter. He and Arthur Anslyn became Commissioners. I remember overhearing my mother telling my father that he could vote for Anslyn if he wanted to but she was voting for Matthew as he could do something for her children. My old lady had known her politics you hear!!! He remained on as Commissioner for twelve years until 1963. He served a total of 20 years as a Member of the Island Council from 1951 to 1967 and from 1971 to 1975.

During his term as Commissioner the road was built from The Bottom all the way to the airport. The schools in both The Bottom and Windwardside were al so built, the hospital on St. John's and so on. The road work provided much employment as it was all do ne by hand. Saba before 1951 had received very little assistance from colonial headquarters on Curacao. In the old representative system a few voters elected two men to advise the Administrator of the Island on budgetary matters. Some of the local councilors stand out for very good proposals they made on how to improve the island. The local councilors were always advocating for a wharf to be built and an attempt was made in 1934 but functioned more as a lookout point than a real wharf as not enough money had been granted to complete the job. Also local councilor Errol Hassel l was able to divert money on Saba's budget in the nineteen thirties to start a "real" road in 1938 from Fort Bay to The Bottom which included the famous S-curve. However it was up to the goodwill of the Dutch colonial Governor on Curacao to approve budget proposals from Saba. His job was to keep expenses as low as possible and it was only perhaps because of an oversight that Errol's ten thousand guilder proposal passed the Governor's attention.

From the time Saba was settled by Europeans in the early sixteen hundreds until well after World War II, the island functioned as an independent nation. All officials were local people, mostly unpaid and even when the island had nearly 2500 native residents the budget was around twelve thousand guilders a year, most of which was brought up locally from some import duties. With the exception of the historian M. D. Teenstra who visited Saba in 1829 when my great-great grandfather Richard Johnson was the Governor, the island saw few if any Dutch officials until the beginning of the 20th century. Nowadays a Dutchman comes in today and tomorrow is telling the Saba people their business and pretends to know it all better than us who have survived here for fourteen generations. Imagine! It is only when Saba started real elections with everyone allowed to vote that progress came. It came about because all the politicians on the various islands were obliged to deliver. Saba as part of the Windward Islands Territory also played a role in the development of St. Maarten. Mathew was sent on many missions for St. Maarten to Curacao in the nineteen fifties. We used to tease him how Prime Minister Efraim Jonckheer's white dog had bitten him when one night Mathew jumped the fence to carry a message from Claude to the Prime Minister. In the process of helping St. Maarten, Mathew was accused of accepting crumbs for Saba. However compared to what we had before 1951, the funds coming in to Saba after that were a big boost for employment. Mathew considered one of his biggest accomplishments the building of the Juancho Yrausquin airport. He said that a Dutchman had told him that an airport might be possible at Flat Point but that it would cost too much. Of course a Dutchman would say that. They still do. Mathew said he would not take no for an answer, so he asked his friend the contractor Jacques Deldevert if he had any ideas. Deldevert was a good friend of Remy de Haenen who later became Mayor of St. Barths.

Remy was a daredevil, had landed on several of the surrounding islands and even had an airport on the island of Tintamarre. Remy had already scouted out Saba for a possible landing. He had already landed here in 1946 with a sea plane and had flown around the island numerous times. Remy came to Saba and they came up with a plan. He asked Mathew to get the land cleared and he would attempt a landing.

The land of course had owners, much of which was owned by my father's family where the runway is and so on. Everyone was interested to cooperate in the interest of the island. Mathew was a man who never took all the credit for himself. I have often heard him praise Eugenius Johnson saying:" If it was not for Eugenius I could not have gotten through. It was he who got permission from the owners of the land and mobilized the people to go down to Flat Point and clear the land so that pilot Remy de Haenen could land". Despite rumors that the Administrator was against the risk of landing a plane and had even threatened to arrest Mathew if anything went wrong, the landing was a success and the airport made a huge difference in the lives of Sabans and those who since then have come here to live.

Of course just like the Commissioners now get unfair criticism to the point that one has to ask where the venom is coming from and why, Mathew also had many critics. He was even given a vote of no confidence in 1962 by the Island Council. A motion which he survived as the rules were different then and he was able to prove with a letter signed by the Administrator that the sloop the "Gloria" was in his father's name and not his. Despite much criticism and some of it very unfair, he kept his calm. He would always tell me that when I was going with him on his sloop to go to school on Curacao he would admire me with so many pens in my pocket. I still carry many pens in my pocket. Even when I go to church I don't feel dressed unless I have a number of pens in my pocket. Politically I was his opposition and in 1971 my party won the elections on Saba. Mathew and I maintained a respectful relationship all our lives. I would give him more credit in this case, as I was a firebrand and a name caller myself, and when I matured I regretted many of the things which I had said about him and other politicians and I would now admit that in his last years we actually became good friends. A speech that I made on his 80th birthday in the Anglican Christ Church in The Bottom was well received by him. So much so that when the main road in The Bottom was named in his honor by my government, he insisted to Commissioner Roy Smith that he wanted the exact same speech made for the occasion. Of course Commissioner Smith had to make his own speech, but I can assure you that Mathew was not amused. Although Roy made a good speech for the occasion Mathew told me on a number of occasions: "Man Roy mess up the thing." And when he passed away I was asked by the family to honor him with a eulogy and I used most of the speech he liked so much also for the eulogy. He was honored with a Medal in Gold by her Majesty the Queen, and he was also honored by the Lions Club of Saba and St.

Maarten. The greatest honor which he could not witness though was when he died on St. Maarten many of the prominent people on St. Maarten came over with the body to pay their respects and he was laid to rest next to the World War II monument in The Bottom. In my book 'Dreaming Big" I honored him and Eugenius Johnson for the role they had played in the early years of representative government on Saba. They opened the road for all future politicians to follow and before they passed away both of them gave me frequent advice on how to go about doing things for Saba.

Mathew Levenston in one way or the other touched the lives of all of us living on Saba today. His generation never had the opportunities which the young people have today. Mathews's generation had to work in order to survive and they did so with pride and dignity. Despite his limitations in the educational field Captain and Commissioner Mathew Levenston succeeded in doing great things for Saba, and also for St. Maarten where he resided as well and shared his time between the two islands.

Abram Simmons

He was the third child born to the marriage of Abraham 'Braw' Simmons (1832-1871) and Elizabeth 'Mam' Horton (1799-1882). His siblings were Joseph Horton, Johanna (married to Thomas Charleswell Vanterpool), and Mary Ann 'Sis' Simmons.

He met Elizabeth Sara Francis Pitt (1835-1895) from Pembroke, Bermuda whom he married on October 22nd 1857. They established their home in "Victoria Cottage" where they had the following children: Walter Irwin, Edgar Freeman, Leyland Scott, Abraham Winfred, Anita Horton and Jerome Simmons.

In the 1860's Abram was the Captain on the schooner "Thrasher" which made regular trips between Bermuda and Demerara, British Guiana with cargos of fresh Bermudian produce. One of the crewmen on many of these trips was John Thomas Pitt Jr. the younger brother of Abram's wife Elizabeth.

We found a press release of Abram Simmons in the December 12th 1871 issue of the Bermuda newspaper the "Royal Gazette" where the following article appeared; LOSS OF THE BRIGANTINE 'JABEZ'.

"It becomes our extremely painful duty to announce the loss on the 25 November last, at Cape Canso, Nova Scotia of the Brigantine "Jabez", Capt. Simmons of these islands, with all her passengers and crew, with the exception of one of the latter....we have received the following: Cape Canser, Nova Scotia 28th Nov. 1871 ..... of the loss of the Brigantine "Jabez", Capt. Abram Simmons from Charlottetown (Prince Edward Island), bound to Bermuda, on the night of the 25th Nov. At Fox Island, about six miles from here... there were ten on board eight men and two passengers...whom we have buried in our Protestant burying ground (cape Canso, Nova Scotia) at two this afternoon (28 Nov. 1871).

"The 'Jabez' was anchored at Port Mulgrove in the Straits of Canser, and during a very severe gale (one of the worst we have had for many years, and bitterly cold), she dragged out of the Strait on the evening of the 25th – the foremast was cut away which took with it the bow sprit; they did this in hopes that the vessel could ride out the gale, but she continued to drag clear across the bay – a distance of perhaps twenty miles ..until she struck the Bar...the mainmast was then cut away, the vessel then drove over the Bar, when the anchors brought her up a few hundred yards from shore...a heavy sea swept away the house forward...taking with it six men, all of whom drowned. All died except the crewman Manuel. The Captain died only half an hour previous to Manuel's rescue. Among those who died was a young man named Stanford Linzey, about 19, from the Island of Saba." Our captains always had sailors from Saba wherever they went.

ON BARGES AND DREDGES

This chapter is dedicated to the unsung heroes who from powerful dredges, opened the ways for many larger vessels, cargo and military ships, from the Panama Canal to the ports of New York and all over Europe. As schooners, steamers and very large cargo and container ships grew, their dimensions imposed additional challenges and navigation risks.

In the past, when dredging equipment was not yet invented, mighty and prosperous harbor cities and civilizations declined and died. Only very rich towns could afford to invest in costly measures to solve their problems of navigation channels.

Amsterdam, for instance, became an important and wealthy town thanks to its international harbor trade. The port was situated on an inland sea, the "Zuiderzee," a shallow bay of 4 to 5 meters, off the North Sea in the northwest of the Netherlands, which was bounded by a closure dam in the year 1932. In front of the entrance to the port a muddy shallow, called "Pampus," was generated by siltation.

The Captains, mates and seamen operating the dredging equipment can be called the unsung heroes of maritime navigation. Without their hard work, the ever-growing vessels would have not been able to pass into a variety of channels and sea passages such as the Suez and Panama Canals or major ports on the South-East coast of USA, and Europe.

Saba's history and culture is wet with the waters of the sea and rivers of the world. Our people left their homes to find occupations linked to the sea whether to Barbados, Bermuda, the Unites States or wherever. Whether as a ship chandler in Portland, a purchaser of ships in Providence, captains and owners of a fleet of schooners on Barbados, wherever they went they trusted the sea to provide them with a living.

Over the past fifty years or more, several of our Saban immigrants to the USA went into the dredging industry to which they were introduced by Leonidas Johnson of The Bottom via the Laborers' Local Union 25.

This is a very specialized industry requiring investment in purpose built equipment of all sizes, designed and constructed to meet a wide range of requirements.

Dredging resources are used to:

• Deepen and maintain waterways, shipping channels, and ports.
• Create and maintain (re-nourish) beaches.
• Excavate new harbors.
• Reclaim land.
• Restore aquatic and wetland habitats.
• Excavate pipeline, cable and tunnel trenches.
• Etc.

The dredging industry has always been an important operation, in particular with the growth of large schooners and merchant ships of great cargo capacity. They are tasked with keeping rivers and sea channels open to ever increasing in size cargo, cruise and military ships, moving goods, people, fuel, etc. The work entails bottom drilling in some instances to determine class of material to be dredged and different types of heavy equipment and machinery geared to drilling hard bottom material such as rock formation and blasting, various sizes dredges and types such as bucket dredges, clam shell dredges and hydraulic dredges using different size discharge lines (up to 36") to move the material churned by using huge cutter heads at the business end of the dredge and pumped through pipe line to form additional land mass, to raise coastal elevation or dump sites, thus different types of dredges for different tasks.

The task involves survey work and laying out the job sites to maintain a specific level of control and specifications required by civil engineers and officials of all parties involved: the contractor, government, and local authorities. The crane operators and mates, usually on eight-hour shifts, are responsible for the supervision of how the tasks are carried out. On board maintenance, the constant repairs and tasks due to usage, not forgetting the high tension on cables and moving parts of course attentive to job specifications, such as depth, marine cables and overhead power lines, telephone lines, working around and under bridges and tunnels etc.

Dredge Alaska had several Sabans operators aboard

The latter in particular is a scary and dangerous proposition, as excavating the sea or river bed passing over a tunnel requires special attention to detail and precautions by all of the involved parties. Those long 100 ft x 4 ft spuds, each weighing 90 to 100 tons each, could cut through the top of tunnel like a hot knife to butter and result in a calamity of huge scale. The process is slow and done very carefully, with no room for error. Milton Johnson mentioned an account where he sweat it out on the Manhattan side when the Battery Park land extension project took place, by Weeks Dredging Contracting Co, the dredging contractor. Those long spuds serve to maintain a stable position while the excavation (digging with a 70 cubic yard bucket) takes place and then the operator using controls in the control cab raises the forward port and starboard spud up off the sea/river bottom, the stern spud using a hydraulic pressure ram pushes the dredge forward then the crane operator lowers the forward port and starboard spuds, followed by raising the stern spud and lowering that to an upright position and excavation process then continues. Meanwhile sounding by the survey crew determines the level and depth of the excavation taking into account the tide. This provides you some idea how this meticulous work is performed.

In some cases, huge barges called 'scows' are delivered alongside the barge by tug boats, each capacity 7,000 cubic yards. Deck winches, using three steel cables, hold the scows alongside and moves forward or backward using the powerful deck winches as the operator dumps the excavated material in the scows, hence keeping a balanced load on the scow. Because of the rocking motion when the crane swings from side to side, this puts a lot of tension on those cables and also the cables that close and raise the clam-shell bucket, in addition to moving heavy equipment, sea, tide and inclement weather all factors, and risks for injuries or death are constant.

I'm not certain that any Sabans are still employed in the dredging industry anymore but they did work on the Panama Canal, Arturo Hassell and Saba Captain a Hassell related to deceased Norman Hassell, canal, rivers, harbors, ports and navy bases of the south-east coast and yes the Caribbean all the way to Lake Maracaibo and Puerto Cabello in Venezuela. They made a living working as members of a union, Local 25, Operating Engineers, Marine division which had a large jurisdiction in by itself, from Maine to Florida. To name a few of the Sabans who worked on barges, the late Norman Hassell's uncle, also known as Norman Hasell, Leonides Johnson, Edmund Johnson, Morris, Richard Henry, Lenous 'Red' Johnson, Henry Johnson, Garvice Johnson, Thomas Johnson, Eric M. Johnson Sr., Phillip Zagers, Cyril Hassell, George Johnson and a few others from the Dowling branch from St. Johns, Saba.

BIBLIOGRAPHIC REFERENCES

Naval History & Heritage Command, Washington, DC.

Bauman, R. (2000). *Awe-Full Moments: Spirituality in the Commonplace.* iUniverse.

Crane, J. G. (1987). In *Saba Silhouettes.* Vantage Press, Inc.

England, G. R. (2008, March 19). *U.S. Department of Defense.* Retrieved 2012, from Office of the Assistant Secretary of Defense (Public Affairs): http://www.defense.gov/Speeches/Speech.aspx?SpeechID=1309

Fenger, F. (1917). *ALONE IN THE CARIBBEAN.*

Hickam, H. H. (1996). The Friday the 13th Patrol. In *Torpedo Junction: U-Boat War Off America's East Coast* (pp. 79-81). US Naval Institute Press.

Hill, A. J. (2010). *Under Pressure: The Final Voyage of Submarine S-Five.* Simon and Schuster.

Johnson, W. (2012). *Tales from my Grandmother's Pipe: A History of Saba by Sabans.* Artygraphic.

Johnson, W. (n.d.). *Facebook.* Retrieved from Of Saban Descent: https://www.facebook.com/pages/Of-Saban-Descent-Saba-Netherlands-Antilles/274049858685

Kol, H. v. (1904). *Naar de Antillen en Venezuela.* Leiden: A.W. Sijthoff.

MacGregor, D. R. (2001). *The Schooner: Its Design and Development from 1600 to the Present.* Naval Institute Press.

University, P. (n.d.). Retrieved from http://www.princeton.edu/~achaney/tmve/wiki100k/docs/

Index